TEDBooks

When Strangers Meet

How People You Don't Know Can Transform You

KIO STARK

TED Books
Simon & Schuster
New York London Toronto Sydney New Delhi

TEDBooks

Simon & Schuster, Inc.
1230 Avenue of the Americas
New York, NY 10020

First TED Books hardcover edition September 2016

For information about special discounts for bulk purchases,
please contact Simon & Schuster Special Sales at 1-866-506-1949
or business@simonandschuster.com

For information on licensing the TED Talk that accompanies
this book, or other content partnerships with TED, please contact
TEDBooks@TED.com.

Interior design by: MGMT. design
Jacket design by: MGMT. design
Illustrated by Julia Rothman

Manufactured in the United States of America

10 9 8 7 6 5 4 3 2 1

Library of Congress Cataloging-in-Publication Data is available.

ISBN 978-1-5011-1998-9
ISBN 978-1-5011-1999-6 (ebook)

For my mother

CONTENTS

When Strangers Meet

The butcher's counter is so high that to catch the eye of the man who makes the sandwiches I have to stand on tiptoe. I order, he nods. When I step back I hear a voice from above me. "How are you?" the butcher asks me from his restocking ladder. "Not bad," I say. "I'm going to be a lot better when I eat that sandwich." He laughs, and turns back to the cans on the shelf.

"And how about you?"

He turns back around. "Me? You came in, my day is made." He bows and smiles. He means it as a compliment and I decide to take it that way. "You have the day off?" I'm not dressed for an office. I can see why he asked.

"Well, I'm a writer, so I'm going to sit at my computer." I make a typing motion. He asks what I'm working on.

"It's a book about talking to strangers."

"You don't say! That's neat." He steps down off the ladder. "You know, I do that all the time. I mean here, sure, that's my job. But everywhere else too." He's spreading his hands in the air, the whole city, he's showing me. "You know, in an elevator or something, not all the time, it's not always right. But just hello or good morning. The other day I'm in an elevator and I say to the woman next to me, I look at her and say just 'Good morning' and then I look back at the doors. I don't want her to think I want anything from her, that's not what it is. So she turns to me, says, 'And good morning to you.'

Then she says, 'You know, thank you. Now I feel like a human.' I just try to do it. I mean, I wish everybody knew. People don't have to live like that, like we're not all right here together."

Talking to people I've never met is my adventure. It's my joy, my rebellion, my liberation. It is how I live.

Here's why. When you talk with strangers, you make beautiful and surprising interruptions in the expected narrative of your daily life. You shift perspective. You form momentary, meaningful connections. You find questions whose answers you thought you knew. You reject the ideas that make us so suspicious of each other.

• • •

I've been thinking about this for a long time. It's not just that my own interactions with strangers resonate with meaning for me. I'm also fascinated with the lives of others, with how people the world over talk to strangers, why they do and why they don't. In the past decade, my fascination has also extended into the networked world, full of new technologies that have the potential to generate new forms of connectedness. Many of the ideas you'll encounter here took shape in a university course I created at NYU's Interactive Telecommunications Program, where I taught technologists and programmers and app designers to understand how the strangers they seek to bring together actually behave, and why people do what they do in the face of people they don't know.

In these pages we'll explore why talking to strangers is good for you. We'll investigate how it's possible for people to open themselves to even the briefest conversations with strangers and the fascinating dynamics of how they do it. What does it take to say a simple hello to a stranger you pass on the street? How might that interaction continue? What are the places in which you are more likely to interact with people you don't know? How do you get out of a conversation? These sound like easy questions. As you'll see, they are not.

Now, the ground rules.

It should go without saying, but this is a book about noticing things that go without saying, so, just in case:

When I talk about talking to strangers, I am talking about open, respectful, genuine interaction. None of what you'll read here is to sanction or suggest that unwanted, hostile contact—street harassment, in other words—contributes to our sense of belonging and humanity. Talking *at* strangers is a form of violence: catcalls, name-calling, objectifying comments about the bodies of others, mockery, threats veiled by diction and threats made by sheer tone. And not only in the immediate moment—when people regularly come up against these behaviors it trains them not to talk to strangers. As a citizen of the street you have two responsibilities. The first is to be kind and respectful. The second is to loudly protest when you see verbally or physically aggressive street behavior as long as you don't think speaking up will make things worse. Protect the ability of everyone to have positive interactions in public with people they don't know by calling out the troublemakers, the haters, the harassers. Don't do it and don't tolerate it.

This is a book about talking, and it's also a book about seeing, listening, and being alert to the world. I want to show you how lyrical and profound our most momentary connections can be, to broaden your understanding and deepen your perception of people who are strangers to you. I want you to see the invisible mechanics and meanings of street interactions. I want to give you a new way to be in love with the world.

1 Who Is a Stranger?

How do you divide the world into known and unknown?
Stranger is a slippery word—you think you know what it means until you try to account for yourself. It names an idea that invisibly structures your everyday life, what you see, the choices you make, the way you move. Are you ready to see just how slippery it is? Tell me what you mean when you say *stranger*.

I ask this a lot, and almost everything I hear boils down to this wonderfully contradictory list.

- Someone you've only seen once.
- The entire world of people you've never met or encountered.
- All the people who are unknown to you but possibly knowable, the people who you're aware of as individuals in some way, but have never met or encountered in person.
- People you have personal information about but have not met, like a friend of a friend, or a public person.
- A person who doesn't share your context, whether that is ideological or geographical.
- A person you don't have anything in common with.
- Someone who is not part of any group you define yourself as belonging to.

- Someone you can't understand.
- Someone who is a threat.
- Someone you encounter frequently but don't know anything about other than what you can observe.
- Someone whose name you don't know.

When we examine our ideas about strangers, the notion that a stranger is someone to be afraid of often falls away, chalked up to childhood training in "stranger danger" or something gleaned from the media, in contradiction to our lived experiences. Who we think is a stranger is an individual thing. It's also defined by culture and history. The ways we interact with strangers—and so our very ideas of whom they are—can change in response to major events. During major disruptions in our lives, in storms, floods, outages, transit strikes, we suspend our usual expectations and put feelings of community above fear. Ever more frequent terrorist attacks by Islamic fundamentalists around the world have directly increased suspicion of strangers—and have fueled illogical and unwarranted assumptions about what *kind* of stranger poses a threat.

Our concepts of strangers and how we behave toward them also vary by situation. Is it dark, am I alone, am I in familiar territory, am I lost, am I in the minority in this place?

Who counts as a stranger? Who do we greet? Who do we avoid? My four-year-old daughter forces me to ask these questions constantly. My family lives in a city, in an area with residential blocks and commercial streets crossing each other.

As my daughter and I walk around the neighborhood, I watch her sort strangers.

I say hello to most people, and she wants to know why. *Are they our friend?* she'll ask. "No, just a neighbor" might be the answer when it's someone we see often or people who are walking near our house. *Do we know them?* "No, we've never met them." *Why did you say hi then?* "It's just nice to be friendly." I think twice when I tell her that, even though I mean it. And as a woman, I know very well that strangers on the street don't always have such noble intentions. It *is* good to be friendly, and it's good to learn when not to be. But none of that means we have to be afraid.

Our apartment is near a halfway house, and some of the people who live there are hard cases, apparently a little "off" in one way or another. They might be dressed in very shabby or unwashed clothes, or behaving in ways that look like they're high on something. Their speech or body language sometimes puts me on alert for behavior that may or may not be harmless. I feel varying degrees of discomfort about any of these situations, and I want my daughter to see that I make choices—and learn to make her own—about who I greet and how I avoid interacting with someone I think might be unpredictable or unpleasant. I want her to understand an essential distinction in a world of strangers: unpredictable and unpleasant are not by definition dangerous.

On our way to school one morning there was a man in the middle of the block we usually walk down, and he was yelling angrily at the air, stomping his feet and swinging his arms. I said to my daughter, "Let's go another way." She asked, *Why can't we go that way, isn't he our neighbor?* Once a question is asked, it snakes through many others. I had to wonder what made me uneasy and whether or not it was based on good instincts or prejudice I'm blind to. That day, I said, "Well, that man looks pretty upset and I don't want to get too close to him." *Why is he upset?* she asked. "I don't know what's bothering him, but I can tell by the way he's yelling and what he's doing with his body that I don't want to get near him right now." I watched her taking that in. I had sidestepped the shorthand of saying, "He's acting crazy," though that's what I would have said to an adult. I wasn't being delicate about my choice of language as much as I was avoiding a cascade of questions I wasn't prepared to answer there on that street corner. What's *crazy*? How did he get that way? Is he always crazy? How do I know someone is crazy?

What was important to me in that moment was that she learn to perceive, not learn to name or categorize.

That's an uphill battle, because categorizing is something human brains do. We categorize people as a shortcut to learning about them. We see young, old, white, black, male, female, stranger, friend, and we use the information we store in that box, the box labeled OLD or FEMALE or STRANGER to define them. Sometimes that's the best we can do, but it creates a dreadful lack of knowing at the individual level.

Categorization and its malignant offspring, stereotyping, are learned at home, in school, on the street. These ways we have of seeing each other also have deep roots in human history. The blunt argument made by some academics (and further oversimplified by the media) says we became hardwired for this in an early moment in human evolution, when having a strong sense of "us and them" helped humans in an extremely resource-poor environment choose who to help and who to exclude so that their group had a better shot at survival. In other words, fear and bias were once useful. It may be in one way or another true that we were once dependent on keeping our groups closed. But turn your most suspicious eye on theories that say humans are hardwired for anything. Someone may be using an idea as a sledgehammer. That word is trying to tell you there's something we can't change. The fact that "us and them" thinking has long roots in human history does not mean that it is natural, or acceptable. It does not mean bias is inevitable and immutable, or that fearful and defensive instincts should continue to drive us.

There's no question: We have to choose whom to trust. The world is full of dangers, and a few of them arrive in the form of an unfamiliar face. We have to navigate that world safely somehow. We can make these choices with attention and grace. If we don't, we will find ourselves in a one-dimensional world, deprived of honest human connections and interruptions that awaken us.

None of this is easy. To learn to truly see someone you've never met is hard. Slotting them into categories is a lazy short-cut we rely on too often. Relying on your perceptions—giving careful attention to what your senses are telling you without jumping to conclusions—costs time and effort. It's not a light-ning reflex but a skill to be learned. You can practice it in places with low stakes. Take a walk in the park, in daylight, and look at the people around you. What do you see? What puts you at ease or sets you on edge? Who counts as a stranger?

Whatever you find, and wherever you think it comes from, one thing is certain: we are surrounded by individuals, not categories. There are adventures to be had here, adventures you can set out for every day of your life. To really understand how you divide the world, to use your senses to choose whom to make familiar, and to stop and say hello to a stranger, these bold acts can transform your emotional experience of the public world. And you can transform the public world itself right along with you.

2 Fleeting Intimacy

This if nothing else: Talking to strangers is good for you. Talking to a stranger is, at its best, an exquisite interruption of what you were expecting to happen when you walked down the street or rode on a bus, shopped at the grocery store or wandered around a museum, whiled away some time on a park bench or waited in a long, slow line. When something unexpected happens it calls you to full attention, turns your awareness outward to the world. You are *awake*. When you interact with a stranger you're not in your own head, you're not on autopilot from here to there. You are present in the moment. And to be present is to feel alive.

You are also connected. Conversations with strangers fill an essential need, one you might think only people you know can fill.

The name of that need is intimacy. When people don't have the makings of intimacy in their lives—a sense of connection, of belonging to some form of community, of closeness to others—they suffer. The relationships we usually call intimate are with family, friends, romantic attachments, mentors, and confessors. The people we know as well as ourselves, the people we see often and miss when they're gone, the people who make us feel at home. This kind of closeness is a long, taut thread that ties us over time.

But the need for intimacy casts a wider net than you might think. There is another kind of intimate relationship, one that holds us together for just a fleeting moment and then vanishes. Its brief and bounded nature takes nothing away from the reality that an intimate moment has been shared: unguarded, honest, with meaningful interior echoes. This is street intimacy. You find it, when you're lucky, by talking to strangers.

If intimacy is private, street intimacy is public. It's a nod of acknowledgment exchanged on the sidewalk, a glance held or a quick "hello" when you sit next to someone on the subway, a parting "take it easy" to the last person getting off the elevator before you do. You find it in all the places people who don't know each other cross paths in passing.

A friend of mine, thirty years ago, was on a train stuck in the station, looking out the doors. Another train pulled up across the platform, and it too went nowhere. She held the gaze of a man on the other train for the long seconds their trains held still. As the doors closed, they waved to each other. The interaction was so emotionally moving for her that she remembers it to this day. For her, it was a moment of connection with a stranger that felt real and good. They didn't need to know each other. Just being human was enough.

You see, it doesn't take much. A shared glance or an exchange of what seems on the surface to be inconsequential patter can make you happy or etch itself into your memory. What's happened is that your existence as a person has been noticed and spoken to. You have been seen.

Ritualistic things we say in passing that we don't really mean

much by, like "How are you?," "Good morning," "Nice day, isn't it?," "Take it easy," "How you feelin'?," "Hi, *mami*," "*Cómo estás?*," these phrases are known to linguists as phatic communication. They're things we say that have little semantic value—we're not really communicating anything factual or necessary. What they have is tremendous social value. These meaningless meaningful words are used between strangers as well as between people who are close. What we mean when we say those things is this: I see you there, hello. These mere acknowledgments carry genuine pleasure and togetherness. We don't want a real answer, we're affirming each other's existence—and that is no small thing.

You can choose to make such simple acknowledgments a habit, and that choice can change you. When experimenters asked a group of customers at Starbucks to either talk to the barista as if they were an acquaintance or to refrain from talk, the ones who made conversation left with positive feelings. Similarly, people on a commuter train were asked to talk to strangers (or not), as were people in the waiting room of an experimental psychology lab where they believed they were in limbo for an experiment to begin. The results of these experiments demonstrated to the researchers that, in general, people feel good when they talk to strangers—*even* if they expect not to. Think about how extraordinary this is: These fleeting connections, what scholars call "minimal social interactions," leave us with such real feelings of connectedness that they actually contribute to fulfilling the basic human need for sociability.

It's Valentine's Day and the subway is full of people who look either sad or happy, no one is indifferent. I squeeze in the middle seat next to a short, round guy with doe eyes and a shaved head. He adjusts a little, but he's still got half my seat.

"I'm sorry," he says, in the gentlest voice. "I'm getting off at the next stop and I'm really uncomfortable, that's why I'm still sitting like this all spread out."

"It's okay," I tell him. "I've got enough room." I've turned and looked him in the eye. I'm smiling. It's really all right. For some reason I want him to know that.

He looks at me a moment. "You know, I don't have a valentine, and that's okay. At my age, I realize that love is my valentine. Just love. You can share love with your family, your aunt, your brother, your pet, your cousin, you can share it with everybody."

"You can share my seat," I tell him.

"See, it's beautiful, right? Happy Valentine's Day," he says, rising as the train slows its way into the station.

•   •   •

The Skin of the Self

As much as cities are shot through with chances to connect in passing moments, they are also full of noise and tension and crowds, of insults and injuries, of people who don't see each other. Street intimacy is special precisely because it is unexpected and far from automatic. City dwellers aren't primed for it. When you walk out the door, you toss your coat on and with it you cover your inner life with a protective shell. It's a thin, invisible boundary that keeps the soft parts of your self safe from people you don't know. Without it, the vulnerability is too great. Just because someone is near you, or interacting with you by necessity, that doesn't mean you owe them access to your inner life. We have contradictory desires. We want to be seen and we want not to be seen. We want to be known and we want not to be known. In every interaction we have, the thickness or thinness of that boundary is negotiated over and over. We close and we open, open and close.

Sometimes when you talk to a stranger it seems that you've gotten more than a dose of their small talk, you've gotten a real glimpse of their inner self. And part of the pleasure is getting that glimpse. The front we present to strangers is a delicate membrane that sometimes can be pierced and sometimes can't. And sometimes in the act of trying, you get through anyway.

I come here a few mornings a week. The clerk knows my face. Today I'm waiting for a bagel, and my phone rings. I have a brief, breathless logistical conversation and then hang up. The clerk looks up and asks me how I'm doing.

I decide to be honest since he's just witnessed the flurry on the phone. "I'm a little frazzled," I tell him. "How are you?"

"I'm fine, thanks," he says, and looks out the window.

I wait until his attention strays back to me. "Would you have told me if you weren't?"

He's confused. "I'm fine," he says again, smiling.

"I know, but if you weren't fine, would you have told me that?"

He laughs at me. It's a laugh I've heard before, the one he reserves for the florid and broken halfway-house residents from around the corner who count out their pennies for coffee. "Of course not," he says, still smiling. "I wouldn't tell you that."

This started as a ritual greeting. I broke the rules and made space to be recognized. I tried to get beneath the surface of his routine chatter into something deeper, and in refusing me, the clerk showed me something anyway. His limits, his privacy, the skin he pulls around himself in talking to strangers all day. He showed me he didn't owe me access to his feelings just because I was asking for it.

•   •   •

The general sentiment.

Listening

I once spent a horse-racing season interviewing old gamblers at the track in Miami. Between races, one of the men put his hand on mine and thanked me. He told me his grandchildren didn't want to hear a word of these stories. He told me about scams and cons and how to read the betting sheet, about the dazzling gangsters whose daughters he guarded. Fantastic stories, funny, illicit, self-incriminating, self-mythologizing, and deftly told. I did almost nothing to earn them. He pulled another seasoned gambler over to meet me. "She's like a sponge, she wants to know everything," he told the man. It was just that. I sat still. I looked at his face. I listened to him. It turns out people don't listen to each other very much. Once someone feels listened to, they can't stop talking.

"Talking to strangers is basically why I moved to New York City. I do it all the time," a young man in a café told me when I said I was writing this book. He had come from a sophisticated but small midwestern town a year ago. "I wanted to give myself the opportunity to be surprised." I asked him what his interactions were like. "It's all about telling stories. For me to tell mine, sometimes. And to get theirs." We shared a conspiratorial nod, he and I, who would never see each other again.

On the radio, there's some talk show banter going on. A new study says men who kiss their wives every morning live five years longer than the ones who don't.

The driver says to me, "I'd kiss my wife every morning if she'd let me!" He's got a sweet laugh. A small guy, bundled against the cold. He touches his chin. "In fact, this morning I told her this was her last chance to kiss my smooth cheek until summer. I'm gonna grow a beard to keep warm. Never had a beard before but I gotta do something, I freeze in these cars."

"Did she kiss you?"

"Yeah, she's a good girl, my wife. We couldn't be more different. She reads books all the time. I don't touch the stuff. I never even went to high school, but somehow we get along real good."

We're driving along the river, traffic is slow. "I met her in the car. A customer. I picked her up by the hospital and we talked so much I forgot where I was supposed to be driving her! She said that was all right. We had breakfast the next couple of mornings and then she moved in. Eight years.

"I grew up over there," he says, pointing across the river to a row of project towers. "I started dealing drugs when I was twelve. I tell you, drugs gave me a good life. I had money. I went all over the world. I went places I don't remember going but people tell me I was there.

"Then I had to get cleaned up. My clock ran down. So here I am." And then he paused. I wasn't sure if there was more. "I'm doing okay. I work, people work."

This looks sad on the page but it's not, he's not. He is laughing that sweet laugh again. He is, I find out later, dying slowly of the things you would expect from the life he revealed. His liver, he says, but not his heart.

In the past few years sociological and psychological studies of how well friends or couples communicate compared with how well strangers do have been reported in the mass media with great lamentation. The studies get interpreted as showing that people who are close communicate poorly, suggesting that some cultural shift has watered down our intimate bonds and brought bleakness to our domestic lives. But to me, those studies entirely miss the point. What they demonstrate is how meaningful and intimate our interactions with strangers actually are. How this special form of closeness is something we need as much as we need our friends and families. We communicate emotionally with our partners because we are close to them, we seek to understand and be understood. But we also rely on a "closeness bias." We assume our partners already know what we mean, that they can read our minds a little, and we want that. We may communicate emotionally more fluidly with strangers because we *don't* assume they already know what we mean. With someone we don't know, we have to start from scratch. We have to explain everything. We tell the story, we explain who the players are, how we feel about them, we spell out all the inside jokes. And guess what? Sometimes they do understand us better.

We also have nothing to lose when we talk about our feelings and opinions and secrets and stories with strangers. We can be vulnerable and share openly with no consequences. If the stranger thinks poorly of us, is shocked, or disagrees, it doesn't matter. A stranger can listen to your feelings without having to live with them.

And here's where it gets even more interesting. If a stranger listens to your feelings, they're also more likely to open up. Vulnerability and disclosure—the sharing of facts, opinions, anecdotes, and emotions that create and deepen our bonds to each other—have their own special logic, a logic of reciprocity. A recent study explored the contours of this dynamic and concluded that "disclosure begets disclosure." If you share merely factual information with someone, it doesn't trigger that mechanism, but when you talk about intimate feelings, about strong beliefs, about barely explored passions, a striking reciprocity takes over. This makes sense when you're with friends, family, and partners. You share, they share. But it works exactly the same way between strangers. If you've ever developed an unexpectedly quick rapport in a conversation with a stranger, disclosure logic is at work.

Easy emotional rapport can also begin with the body. People in general tend to mimic each other without realizing it, and they do it more when they're seeking to be liked. It has become part of dating wisdom that when people like each other, they tend to unconsciously mimic or align their bodily positions, movements, gestures, and vocal expressions. In flirting, whether you're aware of it or not, you attempt to coordinate your body this way in an effort to be liked. In rejecting an overture, you make sure your body isn't in sync to be clear that you're not interested. Experiments have borne out that mimicry communicates (or can be manipulated to communicate) our desired social distance in an interaction. Greater mimicry tells of our desire for greater closeness and vice versa. Researchers call these mimicked bodily movements and rhythms, and synchronized gestures and voices, "embodied rapport." When people feel bodily rapport, it not only leads them to like each other more, it breeds compassion, cooperation, affiliation, emotional support, satisfaction, and even elevated pain thresholds, according to psychological researchers. Embodied rapport also leads people into comfortable self-disclosure.

I'm not just talking about romance here. The unexpected reciprocal openness created by the evidence of the body is just as powerful between strangers in utterly nonromantic circumstances. A research brief to help law enforcement personnel build and maintain rapport in their interrogations detailed how that nonverbal mimicry and self-disclosure by police interviewers turned up more information, more trust, and more cooperation from suspects. Nonverbal behaviors like eye contact, leaning toward the source, and mimicry created physical rapport that opened up disclosure, while self-disclosure by the interviewers elicited reciprocal disclosure from their sources.

Another study demonstrated how physical synchrony leads to embodied rapport and self-disclosure among strangers. Half a group of same-sex pairs were given an abbreviated version of what's now widely known as "the thirty-six questions" that can induce people to fall in love, created by psychological researcher Arthur Aron. The control group worked on editing a document together. Trained observers scored the degree of bodily synchrony and mimicry in each interaction, and the participants were surveyed after their task about their positive emotions and feelings of embodied rapport. They rated things like feelings of closeness or trust, and also things like whether or not there was a "shared flow of thoughts and feelings." And there it was: The greater the physical synchrony, the more significant the disclosure and rapport among the participants.

I know all this and it still surprises me. When I interview people, I quite intentionally engage in bodily mimicry. Interviews are a form of seduction, after all. I align my shoulders, I shift when they shift, I talk at the same speed they do. People open up. They tell me their secrets. And then inevitably, without expecting to, without intending to, I end up sharing feelings I had not yet found words for, or details about my life that few of my friends know. And then they tell me more.

•   •   •

Neighbors

If you live in one place for a while, you start recognizing your neighbors, and the sidewalk intimacy you share is part of what makes that place feel like home. People keep boundaries with neighbors unconsciously, to preserve a sense of privacy and social distance in thickly populated residential areas. Out on the street we form pleasurable, casual bonds with some of our neighbors, we know them and are known by them, we recognize and are recognized. We are anchored in places by the people we know there, by the concatenation of small human transactions that have happened there. These are deep human needs, met by our intimates, sometimes including those who are strangers. They're also met by the people in the neighborhood.

For five years I lived alone in an apartment on a friendly, middle-class, mixed-race city block of apartments and small townhouses bounded at either end by a housing project. People sat on stoops and stood leaning on the gates of their tiny patches of lawn all the time. They pulled weeds and washed cars, walked down to the corner store and back. They spent time on the street and talked to each other.

"Hey stranger" is what my neighbor, the ex-fireman, calls out when I walk by today, but it's been years since we were strangers. I know about the fall that busted his leg, and the pins in his knee that need replacing. I know where he grew up, and that his brother lives across the river. I've admired the hot red Lincoln he stores for the winter, and I helped him out of his plain black sedan once, when his knee was in pain. I know he ran track in high school, cross-country. He chides me on warm days when he doesn't see me in running clothes, and he cautions me to stretch when I arrive home in a sweat.

I told him today that I'm moving. "That's not far, still in the neighborhood," he answered. He shook my hand after all these years and said, "Good luck to you."

"I'll walk by and see you sometime," I told him. It's something you say to someone you might easily never see again, and I'm not even sure which house is his if I wanted to ring the bell. This is street intimacy, I realized, and in a single handshake I saw the boundaries crystallize.

I did walk down the block a few times in the year after I moved, but never ran into the ex-fireman again. The other day I was at a pizza place with my little girl, and she started dancing in mimicry of someone standing behind me. I turned around and it took me a minute to parse the smiling, greeting face. "How you been?" he said. "You remember me?" Of course I did, after my field of awareness shifted to include the block I'd left years ago. I introduced him to my daughter as an old friend, and it felt like the wrong words but I couldn't think of any better. I'd forgotten how rolling and warm his laugh was. The block had gentrified and he'd sold his townhouse, moved out to the beach.

I wrote this book, in some ways, to describe why that moment made me so soaringly happy—why I loved introducing my daughter to a man whose name I could not remember, and calling him my friend.

•   •   •

Strangers Without Bodies

People who make technology have been trying for a long time to connect strangers in the temporary public spaces we enter when we use certain online communities, social media, apps, networks, or games—and it turns out to be very hard. Dating sites and apps aside, because they are built for a narrow purpose with clear communication protocols, I have never seen this done really well. "Site-specific" public projects that put technological communication in the physical world sometimes succeed, like

Branch Out, created by some of my former students, who installed two tall tree-stumplike objects at opposite ends of a park that allow people to talk to each other as if on speakerphone.

The reason I think these attempts fall short is that they take away what is one of the most exciting things about stranger interactions: that they happen when we don't expect them. Part of the fun of talking to strangers is that it's surprising. In physical space, you also swing by your own pendulum about how deeply to engage, from an affirming glance to an emotional connection. These pleasures are hard to reproduce without bodies.

One of the few successes I've seen—and one of my all-time favorites—was Chat Roulette. It worked like this. You turned on your webcam, and the system connected you with another person. You had the choice of using microphones or just text chat, or both. Each of you had the ability to end the connection. If you did, you could get a new connection. At the beginning, there were far fewer exhibitionists and creepy users than you would have expected, and that's when I tried it. The first person the system offered me was a young man in his living room, and we both stayed connected. I was uncomfortable and wildly curious. I told him I was doing research. It was a bit of an emotional dodge, but also honest. He told me he'd used it a few times, found it really fascinating, had had some interesting conversations. He told me what city he was in. I asked if he'd ever exchanged contact information with anyone, or if he would. He said he hadn't, but he might. He wished me good luck with my project. We said good-bye. And that was it—gone, never to be seen again.

One wondrous, unintended pleasure of Chat Roulette was seeing the rooms people were in, bedrooms and living rooms and offices, anonymous, decorated, sometimes obscured. Even if the conversation wasn't deep, seeing the inside of people's houses felt like seeing the inside of their lives. If I talked to people long enough they often took their laptop in hand and gave me a tour of their homes. Teenagers tended to use Chat Roulette in groups. Once a bundle of awkward young teenage boys stopped and looked at me for a moment. "Hey," one shouted, "you must be forty! What are you doing on here?" Then they dissolved in laughter and cut the connection. The most amazing person I talked to was a young programmer in Ukraine. He said his work was very solitary and that he liked to use Chat Roulette to connect with people once in a while for a break. Once, he told me, he got talking with a customer service rep in India, and they ended up leaving the connection open for the rep's entire shift, just keeping each other company without speaking to each other, being, as it were, in the same room.

Other technological approaches to creating an equivalent of street intimacy use tech to generate in-person interactions in physical space. App after app comes and goes (or goes into alpha and looks for funding), trying to create nonromantic "Tinder for strangers in the room with you." They fail for various reasons, only one of which is that they fail to create playful, unexpected interactions. Miranda July's app Somebody (now defunct) was the only one that came close. The app took a playful, performancy turn on creating moments between strangers. The premise was that you could send a message to another person through an intermediary. The messenger had to go find the recipient and speak the message, including any requested physical gestures. The chosen messenger first had to accept the mission and then the recipient had to say it was a good time to receive it. It didn't work very often. The human density of cities makes it likely there will be another user close to your friend. There is also a density of purpose in cities—deadlines and schedules, second jobs and pedestrian errands, constant busyness and little idling—that makes it *less* likely people will be able to take a few minutes away from what they're doing to deliver a message. I never had a message go through, but last year I delivered one. I walked about ten minutes out of my way to a restaurant and found my target. He had told the waitstaff to expect someone looking for him. I went to his table, put my heavy bag down on one of the chairs, and did my thing. Everyone stared. He and his tablemate laughed and clapped. The hard thing was knowing what to do when it was done. Their dinner hadn't arrived yet. The three of us looked at one another warmly. After an awkward minute, I said, "Okay, there you go!" and left the restaurant. I loved that joyously awkward minute. Discomfort always shows an honest hand. We were just three real humans sharing a really weird moment. My companion had hung back at the doorway and watched the whole performance. He said, "You were totally ready to sit down and have dinner with them, weren't you?" I really was. It was strange and wonderful.

Not everyone would think so. When I tell people who identify as introverts about my work on stranger interactions and the idea that it is a pleasure, there's a common response that surprised me until I heard it so often it didn't anymore. Here's a composite of what I tend to hear: "I have so much trouble talking to people in social situations, where I'm supposed to. But I really enjoy things like talking to people who are standing around or walking a dog or working in public, asking them what they're doing, finding out what they know about the world that I don't, or just saying hello." This contradiction in their experience tends to be expressed as a mystery they keep trying to solve.

It actually makes perfect sense if you recognize that those are two different social situations, and the ones the introverts like are the kind of exchange that happens just once. You won't see the person again, or even if you do, you won't be required to pick up the conversation or increase the connection. You don't have to worry about what they might think. You have total control over ending the interaction—you can walk away at any time. You are in the conversation in the first place because of your curiosity. And you enjoy this because it is a pleasure that's separate from relationship-forming conversations, from conversations with expectations, with rituals, with potentially lasting effects. What you're doing is socializing in a different way.

There's a full moon, and a friend texts me to tell me to go out and see it. I do, and down on the stoop I dawdle, looking up. I take a picture, like everyone does now. A woman with lovely curls is walking up the street with her dog. She stops a few doors shy of mine and turns around. She takes a picture too.

"It's a pretty one," I say as her dog starts tugging and she turns back around, walking toward me. She ends up telling me about how she never much went out in the evenings until she got the dog.

"I used to see all my friends' pictures, this moon, that sunset, and I'd say, 'Oh man, I missed it again.' But now," she said, shaking the leash. "I'm out with this dog. I found him in July. Now I'm out every night."

3 A World Made of Strangers

So there is pleasure to be had when you talk to a stranger, a shimmer of connection. Seeking out these experiences not only changes your everyday experience, it can also have an effect on the larger political world, leading us away from fear and building toward openness, cooperation, and genuine understanding.

Tremendous cultural anxiety about dangerous strangers floats through the streets. I am talking here about ideas, about specters, about newspaper statistics, about the plots of movies and novels, about individual experiences that carve spaces in us, and the way experiences flow outward into public conversation.

All this anxiety doesn't come out of nowhere. Historically, real and imagined strangers are figures who embody danger and possibility simultaneously. For most of preindustrial history, the majority of people did not live in cities and thus had little cause to encounter strangers. People crossed paths with strangers at the trading market and on the road. In places where good bargains and ripe swindles were equally possible, the danger was in your pocket. On routes taken by tradespeople and travelers alike, brigands and thieves lay in wait, while the luck of finding safe shelter with strangers, as well as sound advice from them, was equally possible. The occasion of an unknown traveler's arrival in a small village was a big event, and required delicate negotiation. They had to be fed and lodged, without knowing what might come of it. They might be honest people and bring good fortune, buying goods or bearing news. They might be thieves. Or one posing as the other. You see these dualities distilled in European fairy tales. Imposters, bandits, untrustworthy old ladies, the Big Bad Wolf on the road. And then there are the stories of humble youngest sons who set out to find their fortune. On the way, they share their scant food with a stranger on the road, and always that stranger gives them things like invisibility cloaks and winning secrets, magic tokens that help them prevail.

Walk forward into the first industrial revolution and then the second. As cities began to expand and fill with factories, things changed. People streamed in from the countryside to fill the factories with ready hands, and the problem of readability became constant and urgent. For the urban middle class, for the newly urban workers, there were new questions. How can we tell who these people are, and how do we know if we can trust them? How do we behave toward them? And later, in the 1920s, women appeared regularly in public spaces, adding another layer of confusion to the way people on the street tried to read each other.

These histories live in us. We know the folk tales, so we know things can go either way. We are still awkward, at best, when we try to understand people who aren't like us. We are suspicious, and sometimes with good reason. We still face the difficulty of confirming that strangers are who they say they are, and the difficulty of reading and trusting their intentions. Most of us live in crowds and move from house to house, neighborhood to neighborhood, city to city, country to country, in search of something better or something new. If we can, we carry identification, for it is routinely demanded of us. We still act as though living among strangers was new to us, was not the norm.

Why are people afraid of strangers? Because their status or intentions can't easily be read. Because crimes and aggressions are sometimes committed by or between strangers and these are the crimes and aggressions we hear about most in the media. Because there are situations in which our ability to read each other does matter materially. It matters to the safety of our bodies, and so our ability to read each other becomes urgent. Because fear is easier than risk.

Without nuanced perception, our fears are a brutal barricade against the presence and openness that could allow encounters with strangers to change us and the world we live in. Fear that is categorical or universal feeds the prejudices that become oppressive laws and unforgiving policies, justifications for social control and everyday violence. So there is more than intimacy at stake when we choose to talk to strangers. Talking to people who are different from us can be radically transformative. It's the antidote to fear.

•   •   •

The more visually familiar something becomes, the more we are likely to feel comfortable with it. The less unfamiliar a type of person or type of face or style of dress becomes, the more likely we are not just to tolerate it, but to actually *like* it. Social psychologists call this the "mere exposure effect" and it's supported by experimental research over many decades.

Let's take a silly example. The more often you see a woman with dyed-green hair, the more likely you are not just to like her, but also to think that anyone with green hair—men, women, black, white, South Asians, the elderly, or the young—must be all right. Or, to raise the stakes, the more often you're in contact with Arabic-speaking women wearing hijab, the more likely you are to feel positively about women wearing a hijab or speaking Arabic. This is the fantastic trick of mere exposure: it is *generalized*. That we have a tendency to like new things or types of faces or types of people who share characteristics with something that's already become familiar to us—that's a potentially world-changing thing. And it's a strong argument for living in diverse communities and talking to strangers you meet.

The more you are exposed to people who are different from you in this loose and generalized way, the more likely you are to like them, and maybe even try to understand them, how they live, and what they believe. For individuals and for the communities, cultures, neighborhoods, and countries in which they live, making a habit of interacting with strangers can be transformative. It can change emotions, ideas, and politics and the tangled places where they overlap. This matters to our social imagination as well as the laws and systems that shape our social world.

The clerk at the neighborhood corner store is a small Muslim woman with a sheer scarf tossed around her neck and covering her head. She likes the red streaks in my hair.

"How do you do it? I do my daughter's with food coloring." She sweeps her hands across her brow and then down by her shoulders. "Her bangs and then the ends. Other daughter wants blue, green. I do whatever they want."

I'm imagining these bright peacocks hidden under veils. "Do they wear veils?"

"No, not at all," she tells me. "That is their choice. I teach them what I want to teach them, what I believe. They have their own brains. They have to choose, or not choose. I can't force them."

She leans forward over the counter, smiles a little. "My son, he wants green hair too." She slides one finger across the counter, a division. "I say no. There is a line."

In the space of this, maybe half a minute, I discovered to my shame that I was thinking categorically about a group of people: women in headscarves in my neighborhood. I assumed she was very religious and would demand that her daughters abide by her own beliefs. In those few seconds, this woman became an individual to me because I talked with her, and saw her, heard her, and learned something about the way she organizes her world.

The act of merely talking to a stranger pushes us to see them as an individual person. Not a body or a category. And that's an incredibly powerful thing. When you experience someone as an individual, it opens up your idea of who counts as human.

And that right there, that small, individual change is a whisper of larger political ones. In the face of our global struggles over refugees and immigration, racism and hatred and harassment, simply seeing someone as an individual is a political act.

•   •   •

Being Cosmopolitan

You might think I'm pegging a lot of weight on the political importance of strangers talking to each other, and I am. I also want to be clear that the path by which chatting on street corners takes on political dimensions is winding and risky and full of blind alleys.

For me it starts with cosmopolitanism, a philosophical concept with origins in ancient Greece and later a political ideal of the Enlightenment. The basic idea is that rather than being citizens of a nation-state, people are citizens of the world, that they identify first as human beings and only second as members of a state, nation, race, ethnic group, affinity group (or several of these concurrently). It is a moral foundation. As cosmopolitans, as humans, when our other identities come into conflict with our shared humanity, shared humanity wins.

In recent years urban planners, sociologists, political scientists, anthropologists, and cultural geographers have been using the idea of cosmopolitanism as they try to hash out how lived experiences of cultural mixing can change social relations, can reduce prejudice, can create solidarity and stronger democracy.

Cities are machines for interaction among strangers, and more than fifty percent of the global population now lives in cities. These new urbanists are working on what can be done in cities structurally and socially to encourage cultural mixing and generate positive contact among people who belong to different social groups. One constant theme in their work is that when people talk to strangers, the interactions enact and nurture tolerance, mutual respect, and understanding. They can be transformative. And that's the point.

Context is the trickster in this story.

To be a cosmopolitan—to be tolerant, open, and curious and believe we are all in this together—takes empathy. You have to be able to imagine yourself seeing and feeling the world from another person's perspective. That means your own internal processes are part of the context.

Empathy, an emotion, is affected by bodily experience. The ability of both humans and mice to empathize is affected by physiological stress levels—the less stress, the greater the empathy, according to a neurological study. If you feel connected to someone—even in a fleeting way—you're more likely to vicariously experience their emotional and physiological states, and to have empathy for them. Our capacity for empathizing with people we don't know, both in the abstract and with individual strangers, is not only based on our own personalities and beliefs. It's situational and variable and can be deeply influenced by our state of mind, by feelings of connectedness or the lack of them.

Empathy is not something you inherit. Throw the idea of human nature out the window here. Empathy is an ability that usually develops in early childhood and is often taught by parents and in schools. It can be fostered or squelched by formative experiences. Empathy can be limited by prejudice.

The way we act toward others on the street—whether they are similar to us or not—also depends on external context. I like how clearly this shows up in a series of experiments about people's willingness to help strangers in public.

The experimental scenarios are:

1. The dropped pen—will a stranger pick up the pen? Will they point out that it has been dropped?

2. The hurt leg—will a stranger help someone injured who is struggling to retrieve something?

3. Change for a dollar—will a stranger make small change? Will they even check to see if they have any so change can be made?

4. The unmailed letter—will a person pick up a stamped, unmailed letter and drop it in a mailbox?

People's willingness to help each other—and by extension their ability to empathize--varies by where they are and who they're being asked to help and under what conditions. Some things that matter according to researchers are local culture, the specific situation, the demographic characteristics of the place, and whether they're in a hurry. In US cities, factors that sway empathetic behavior include the level of income inequality in the area (the less inequality, the greater the inclination to help), the crime levels (unexpectedly, increases in crime correlate to increases in helping), the population density, and typical walking speed. Specific political circumstances and common street behaviors also deeply affect people's responses to someone in need. When these types of experiments were performed in the early 2000s in Kiev, the commonness of pickpockets produced a disinclination to make small change in coins. In Tel Aviv, the fact that unclaimed packages have often been bombs made people unwilling to touch unmailed correspondence, while in Albania postal unreliability made it a futile errand.

How changeable we are as individuals, how situational our empathy and altruism are, all show that it's no easy thing to approach the world with cosmopolitan intentions even when you're trying very, very hard.

Understanding what it's like to be in someone else's shoes, to see the world as they do, is not just a matter between individuals. Perspective is a wide concept. Having perspective also means understanding and recognizing the systems that shape and constrain our perspectives. At an individual level you may be a tolerant and empathetic neighbor, and openly, without prejudice, converse with anyone you pass on the street of any race. But in a country like the United States, where racism is built into the systems of governance and privilege in which we live, I take caution. Cultural geographer Kurt Iveson places an important limit on cosmopolitanism as an ideal. He points out that in our everyday reality, the ability to practice openness is not evenly distributed. To insist that all city dwellers practice radical openness and tolerance has a significantly different meaning for weak groups than for privileged ones that can choose when and where to be open, when and where to engage in cosmopolitan mixing. He reminds us that in some cases "the construction of fragile boundaries which limit engagements with others is all that protects the weak from annihilation—some boundaries and exclusions might well be politically justified." So, if you are someone from a privileged class, you owe it to your social world to practice cosmopolitan behavior. You also shouldn't expect people without your privilege to automatically meet you there. Part of being a good cosmopolitan means living with the fact that, if you are part of a dominant culture, you have benefited from that culture whether you asked to or not.

So, I cannot say to you, "If people talk to strangers, all our urban social problems and cultural discrimination go away." It's infinitely more complex than that and involves so much more than simply changing the way we encounter each other. But when you talk to a stranger, when you admire and respect their differences from you, when you help them, you are making the world around you more malleable, creating spaces for change. What's beautiful is how these moments of possibility are created by small social exchanges. The act of talking to strangers in itself does not solve anything at a cultural or political level. It's far from a solution. It's a start.

•   •   •

Contact and Prejudice

Imagine yourself stepping inside a large golden box and striking up a conversation via full-body video with someone in Herat, Afghanistan; Tehran, Iran; Havana, Cuba; New York, New Haven, or Washington, DC, in the United States, that replicates what it's like to talk with them in the same room. This is exactly the experience had by users of the Portals Project, by an arts and technology collective called Shared_Studios. Inside the Portals, the users talk with people they may have little in common with, and whose governments are sometimes at odds. They talk with people about whom they will certainly have preconceptions and possibly prejudices. Most users come away with positive, moving experiences, and often say they wish there could be a Portal in every country. At the time of this writing, three thousand people have stepped into Portals. Shared_Studios has more than a dozen new Portals planned—they invite requests, and they publish the construction and technology plans for anyone to make their own. The project is both grandiose and compact in its aims. The artful extension of people's ability to interact with strangers far and wide ups the ante for the ways we can extend ourselves as cosmopolitans.

Portals are also unintended machines for social change. Positive individual experiences with people from other groups significantly reduce prejudice in opinions and behavior. Social psychologists call this the "contact hypothesis." Positive experiences with one person reduce your prejudice toward the entire group to which you think that person belongs by a bit of fancy psychological footwork known as member-to-group generalization. More than fifty years of experiments, mostly about US black-white interracial tolerance and antagonism, have demonstrated this over and over. The idea holds sway over the work of governments, local community groups, and other institutions working for social change. If only we could mix things up, the logic goes, everything would be better.

These positive experiences don't have to be perfect, according to the contact hypothesis. It still works if the interaction with someone who is an outsider to your group makes you a little uncomfortable. As long as the interaction is generally friendly and sustained long enough and has a few other qualities defined by researchers, chances are you'll get more comfortable and come away with a good experience overall. If the experience didn't meet the conditions for a positive experience (including time spent)—or if it was openly hostile, of course—no experimenters expected any reduction in prejudice just on the basis of being in contact with someone different. What contact hypothesis studies were not designed to look for was an *increase* in prejudice following negative experiences.

That blind eye explains a lot about the way real-world experiences spill over the lines drawn by experimental evidence. Real-world experience presents a massive contradiction to the contact hypothesis. In the United States, given the desegregation of schools, communities, and workplaces in the past fifty years, given at least some increased interracial contact—you would expect a dramatic decrease in racial prejudice, right?

But both lived experience and the findings of sociological and anthropological research show this is far from the case.

Diverse areas often show the *highest* levels of intergroup tension, prejudice, and conflict. The puzzle created here is seemingly insoluble.

Nobody likes an unsolved riddle. In recent years, researchers have gone back to the hundreds of studies supporting the contact hypothesis to find out what happened as a result of overtly unpleasant experiences. They also ran several original experiments on white contact with blacks in the United States, and white-black and white-Muslim contact as well as contact with asylum seekers in Australia.

What they found is a lesson in futility. The effect of negative experiences dramatically outweighs positive ones in changing the degree of prejudice for the group that person is a member of. Their work, they say, "Suggests that intergroup contact may be naturally biased toward worsening intergroup relations rather than improving them." While positive interactions are much more common than negative ones, the hard blow of a negative experience can easily outweigh many positive experiences. These researchers say that the degree of increase in bias and prejudice depends on the individual's previous experiences with members of that group. They still extend hope that positive contact can make real changes.

So here is the ongoing dilemma: contact and exposure to people who are different from you can breed *intolerance* instead of the happy tolerance so many social psychologists, urbanists, policymakers, activists, and individuals hope and work for. Bad experiences with people from other groups turn out to have disproportionately more power in forming prejudice in ideas and behavior. That's one of the reasons why the increased racial and ethnic integration and coexistence of the past half century seems to have had little effect on intergroup prejudice as a whole, and particularly on the part of whites as a generalized group.

The majority of experiences are positive, but the negative ones sink the ship. The lesson here is that if we want to make social changes, it's imperative that we create an overwhelming density of positive experiences between people who are different, and, as a culture, that we insistently, publicly challenge people who create negative experiences.

You shouldn't be surprised here if I tell you it can also be more complex than just positive or negative. In daily experience, outside the pared-down situations created in lab experiments, things are a little different. Sometimes a single interaction can hold both hopeful and discouraging consequences. People may experience these simultaneous opposites as an alternating current electrifying their days. Sociologist Elijah Anderson's book *Streetwise: Race, Class, and Change in an Urban Community*, about a Philadelphia neighborhood with a black side and a white side, describes the way residents navigate around the boundary and pass through it. There is so much delicate work that goes into tolerant coexistence, and sometimes it comes off nicely. So much of it hinges on people's ability to read each other through difference. One of the men Anderson interviewed tells this story.

He describes how late one night he and a small group of black friends came close to passing by a white woman on the sidewalk. She walked faster and then went up to the porch of a house as if she lived there. It was transparent to the young informant that she was scared of them, and that she didn't live there.

> "Miss, you didn't have to do that. I thought you might think we're some wolf pack. I'm twenty-eight, he's twenty-six, he's twenty-nine. You ain't gotta run from us."

She protests that she was in a hurry. He responds:

> "No you wasn't. You thought we was gon' snatch yo' pocketbook." We pulled money out. "See this, we work." I said, "We grown men, now. You gotta worry about them fifteen-, sixteen-, seventeen-year-old boys. That's what you worry about. But we're grown men." I told her all this. "They the ones ain't got no jobs; they're too young to really work. They're the ones you worry about, not us."

The interaction the man recounted to Anderson seems to end in a smile, a laugh, and a lesson. Then everyone moves on. But it smacks of the limits of contact, too. Anderson draws that line. He writes that encounters like this might change a mind or a fearful behavior, but it's not much in the face of overall prejudice and stereotyping of blacks by whites. Because the lesson is not only taught to the white woman, that her mistake is a misreading, an unnecessary fear, but also to the young men, a vivid reminder that they are consistently read as dangerous strangers simply because they are black.

This thing, this particular misreading, happens a million times a day the world over. It's an ugly thing, a painful one. What stays with me about the young man's story is how he responded. How he stopped and turned a tense and insulting interaction into an honest, awkward one.

I have no rosy vision of everyone having walked away from this interaction happier and more comfortable or in any way fundamentally changed. What I see is that the young man challenged the woman's unspoken and invisible fears, that he named and dismantled her assumptions.

Consider this moment from Claudia Rankine's wrenching, precise, and damning book *Citizen: An American Lyric*. The "you" here is a black woman.

> In line at the drugstore it's finally your turn, and then it's not as he walks in front of you and puts his things on the counter. The cashier says, Sir, she was next. When he turns to you he is truly surprised.
>
> Oh my God, I didn't see you.
>
> You must be in a hurry, you offer.
>
> No, no, no, I really didn't see you.

When you think about talking to strangers and changing the world, one of the complexities is the system you're in and how it might blind you. What weighs down on you as you extend a greeting to someone you've never met and probably never will again? If you want the contact hypothesis to work, if you want to make one of those small moments of possibility, you always have to shine light on what might make it fail.

There's seeing and there's *really* seeing.

4 The Mechanics of Interaction

When strangers meet, in any culture, in any place, in any
social group, the same unasked questions float in the back-
ground: What is appropriate public behavior here? How do we
avoid interactions; how do we get into, conduct, and get out
of interactions? How do we manage our physical and social
distances? How do we choose who to interact with and who to
pass by? How do we communicate our intentions and intuit
those of others?

These are the mechanics of stranger interactions—the phys-
ics problems that need solutions. How to read the schematic
diagram. How to keep the engines, levers, and gears running
smoothly. How to manipulate friction and grease. The solutions will vary depending on what country or culture or affinity
group you find yourself in but the mechanical *problems* do not
vary. The behaviors I describe in this chapter may sound familiar or they may differ wildly from your experience. The point is
to learn about the things that go without saying: What are the
mechanics of interaction in the places where you live and play,
work and pass through?

These mechanics in any community are tacitly agreed
on, unwritten, and not explicitly stated. These agreements
become visible when you observe public behavior and look for
patterns in what people *do*, rather than relying on what people

say about what they do. And just as often when the rules are broken—as they constantly are, in small ways—we see them written in bold ink.

When you look for what goes unsaid, the first thing to understand is the basic degree of sociability people expect in public space. That baseline will vary with the type of space you're in, the occasion, time of day, and the culture, subculture, or microculture. It's a social contract, and like any social contract, we don't think about it when it's kept, but when it's not, we react with anything from annoyance to outrage. This happens within a culture or situation, and it can also happen when communities overlap and their differing implicit contracts are layered over each other in the same locations. The grit in the system of interaction, if there is grit, exposes the points of difference, the implicit rules for each community.

In the late 1950s, renowned sociologist Erving Goffman began to observe and document these rules explicitly. His book *Behavior in Public Places* and other essays in his vast oeuvre are careful analyses of the verbal and nonverbal behaviors and cues that govern interactions among a particular group: the US population of white, Anglo-American middle-class people in that time period. Goffman speaks plainly about the limits of his studies and consistently reminds readers of the constraints and specificity of his observations. He frequently points to stories and studies of rules and patterns of public behavior that differ from his findings in places as far away as India, Latin America, rural Ireland, Kuwait, and France. While his observations are highly specific to a time, place, and demographic group, his investigation builds a structure for making sense of what happens when strangers meet.

Remember that in lived experience, this is a fluid process about which we do not think much at all. We're slowing it down and taking it apart to see how it works.

• • •

Civil Inattention

In the US cities and towns Goffman studied—and many of the other cultures he mentions via the research and anecdotes of others—the baseline contract is what he and sociologists since call "civil inattention." It's a strategy to preserve one's desired social and physical distance, for well-managed social distance is part of what allows us to live comfortably in crowded cities. Think about your relationship with your neighbors—how much physical distance do you have from them and how much social distance do you prefer? Think about the way you choose seats in a theater, or on public transportation. We need some imaginary space in our tight physical and social spaces. Jane Jacobs, a foundational interpreter of city life, said it perfectly: "A certain degree of contact is useful or enjoyable; but you do not want them in your hair. And they do not want you in theirs either."

Civil inattention is something we expect and receive, without thinking much about it at all. It's the grease that keeps the gears turning. Everything goes smoothly. No friction, no bother, not a minute wasted.

Here's what Goffman observed in watching the way unac-
quainted pedestrians manage civil inattention. As two strangers
move toward each other in a public space, they glance at each
other from a distance then avert their eyes as they get closer
and continue to pass by. This little maneuver accomplishes two
things: the visual behavior pattern signals the acknowledgment
of each other's presence in a shared space. The subsequently
averted eyes assert that each has no intention of intruding on
the other, that neither is a threat, nor expects that the other is
a threat. There's no vigilance and no incursion. Their mutual
inattention is decidedly civil.

So, in communities that expect civil inattention, you'll observe vocal and physical conventions that help people stay out
of each other's hair. Whatever the exact signals may be, they
often include a congenial flicker of recognition of each other's
existence without any social engagement, without the feeling
that we are directly observing each other. We acknowledge
that we briefly share space and we preserve distance, we relieve
each other of the necessity for interaction. We declare with our
bodies that we are harmless and don't intend to intrude on each
other. We're not selling anything, we're not asking for anything,
we're not flirting with each other, we're not harassing each
other, we're not a threat.

In some cultures, by contrast, people take extraordinary mea-
sures not to interact at all. A friend explained to me that often
in Denmark interaction with strangers is avoided at almost any
cost. People sitting in an inner seat on a bus or train would go so
far as to miss their stop rather than speak to their seatmate and

ask them to move aside. There's an elaborate physical perfor-mance of shuffling bags and using the body to indicate you need space to get by, all to avoid speaking the words *Excuse me*.

I've been told that Toronto—though not other places in Canada—is similar. Even eye contact is avoided. One person I spoke with told me that "strangers in Toronto talk (or mutter) to each other only when necessary, and with the tacit understand-ing that it's painful for all involved. 'Excuse me' is a last resort on the streetcar." Another Toronto native said the city's "much-hyped 'neighborhood' identities can toss up differences. Here in Cabbagetown, home to many excellent freaks, I sometimes get mildly irritated that the shopping trips involve having conversa-tions with the people behind the counter. I guess that makes me a 'good,' i.e., typical, Torontonian."

A British woman who has lived in the United States for many years reports, "When talking to Brits, I've noticed an inter-esting thing: as I become more (what I think of as) American, and thus willing to say something to a perfect stranger, I have noticed that actually lots of English people respond quite well to that—better than Americans, almost, perhaps because it's so unexpected. But there's a nice thing in England where when you say one thing, it's perfectly understood that you're not starting a conversation, so there's no anxiety."

People from Egypt have reported to me that it's common for people to be curious and open to strangers, excited to get into conversations and learn about them. An Egyptian friend told me she thinks there's actually a premium on strangers because they're a novelty, and they'll have new stories.

The public spaces we share don't always feel as benign as the ones Goffman portrays, and civil inattention can involve larger gestures than a flick of the eye. Elijah Anderson's 1990 book *Streetwise*, about an urban neighborhood that's split down the middle—half black and half white—closely details how recognition and inattention habits are navigated in areas where perceived potential threats are high. In Anderson's territory, that potential threat is felt between black men and also in interracial interactions. For example, beyond the signals of gaze, Anderson saw a pattern of intricate behavior of crossing streets to avoid direct passing on a sidewalk at certain times of day in certain places—both to signal harmlessness and to avoid potential harm, to minimize tension and allay fears.

Inattention may be a baseline, but there are all kinds of reasonable, tolerable workaday interruptions, and sometimes they're even pleasant. Goffman cataloged some of these. When do you feel obliged to interrupt a stranger's path? You might stop someone who has dropped something, or apologize to someone in whose way you have gotten. There are requests that cannot be politely refused, like asking someone for the time, or asking for directions—although you can make sure no one asks you for help by avoiding passing glances completely. People are generally aware when they're stepping slightly out of tune for a good reason and can expect that a well-intentioned overture will be received as such. Genuine and helpful, or at least harmless.

What happens when we're not in motion and the interaction can't naturally end as we continue on our way? In many parts of the United States, people also grant each other inattention when they sit at close quarters in cafés, or on park benches or in picnic areas, at beaches, ballgames, or outdoor concerts and music clubs: places where the expectations can be less cut and dried. Some people want to keep a sense of privacy at close quarters and in parallel activities. The illusion of privacy means they can be comfortable and go about their business. People may choose not to acknowledge each other in these situations, perhaps because it's harder to keep boundaries if we make eye contact or start talking when we're sharing space. By contrast, in western Austria and Switzerland, a woman I interviewed said that when someone walks into a café or any public space with a defined entrance point, everyone says hello, and when anyone exits everyone says good-bye. In between entering and exiting, the clear expectation is that you don't get involved. I like how warm and welcoming that sounds, but when she told me this all I could think was how distracting it would be.

Civil inattention in these situations, the park and the café, the theater and the concert, also amounts to a denial of shared experience. Sometimes that's a terrible loss. Collective experiences are transcendent and oceanic and every culture in history has engineered them, from theater to religious practices to basketball games. I'm not saying you should break expectations and feel deeply moved every time you go to a concert or a picnic in a crowded park, but you might consider being open to it.

Now, what happens when two people share the sidewalk or different groups share a public space *without* sharing the same baseline contract of public social behavior? Behavior in movie theaters, in which the audience is a temporary community, is a brilliant display of how varied and conflicted baseline expectations can be. The overtly advertised expectation in a movie theater is silence and focused attention. The theater's preview sequences specifically point out the rules: phones put on silent or turned off, voices down to a whisper. The degree to which that contract is kept varies widely by what kind of cultural neighborhood the theater is in, by the type of movie, by the general age of the audience, even the time of day (very late shows have looser expectations). In startling or hilarious scenes in a film, even people sticking to the letter of the theater's rules may still break the contract of silence with laughter or shrieks, sharing the heightened emotion in a ritualistic moment that breaks the contract and then ends swiftly. That contract is less and less universal. It's increasingly common to watch a movie in a temporary community that incorporates consistent collective experience and doesn't expect silent, focused attention, despite the theater's stated expectations. In some temporary communities, tweeting commentary on the movie is part of the fun. Black audiences and younger audiences of any race have very different expectations than adult white audiences, in general. Social class also affects expectations, regardless of color. At the movies, all of this has a historical context too. The expectation of silence, of civil inattention in movie theaters began when national movie chains emerged and—in direct contrast to often raucous locally run theaters— banked on the competitive advantage of a touch of glamour and the high-culture expectations of live theater, enforced by both implicit contracts and ushers.

Verbal and even physical conflicts can and do arise when people with different cultural expectations about public behavior share space and are perceived as violating the baseline social contract of each other's place or culture, whether intentionally or not. Black people in any public space that is not predominately black may get stared down and hassled, and treated as threatening no matter what their dress and behavior. White men walking through black housing projects may be stared down and hassled. Loud teenagers in a family neighborhood, or a wealthy one, may face a visit from the cops that, depending on the racial situation, may be extremely dangerous for them. Any of these situations could escalate into a fight. Knowing that the local rules may differ from your own and figuring out what they are and how far they'll bend is important. Anderson separates what he calls street etiquette from street wisdom. The former is a sense of a set of categorical rules that can be spoken and learned, while the latter derives from experience and allows a person to read unfamiliar situations and strangers on an individual basis.

• • •

The Gaze
On the street, in public space, most of the time the goal is to avoid truly intruding on anyone, or frightening them, or causing them any unpleasantness. How do you know if someone is open to verbal contact or not? How do you show that you are or aren't?

The art of talking to strangers demands that we become deft readers of one another and skilled senders of clear messages.

Let's go back to the eyes—this is where it all starts. The gaze is the core of human interaction. Meeting someone's eye can be a powerful statement of openness and inclusion, or of desire or revulsion. Navigating the world of strangers starts with knowing what gazes mean.

In Goffman's study, people who are open to interaction briefly bring their eyes back to their potential interaction partner as they come closer, and hold their eyes momentarily. This slightly prolonged glance is a question and an answer. *Are you friendly? I am.* It's *not* a stare, which can be threatening and invasive and create a snake pit of negative feelings. An open glance is an overture and like any overture it can be rejected. The brevity of the glance lets you save face if it is. Rejection can look like the absence of acknowledgment, decidedly averted eyes, or a cold stare. Acceptance is an opening that can then be met with a nod, a smile, or a passing word.

Again, a reminder: the meaning of gazes varies widely among different cultures—direct eye contact is more common in the United States than, for example, in Japan, and in some cultures and situations direct eye contact is a challenge or an assertion of power. So Goffman's description doesn't apply universally. Gazes always signal something, but openness to interaction is just one thing a gaze can signal.

Our decisions—whether instinctual or conscious—about whether or not we're going to make that gazing overture start with the information we get from our senses and our bodies. We notice the way people dress. We guess their age; we notice their apparent gender, the shade of their skin. We notice the angle of their shoulders, the expression on their face, the speed of their gait, and what they do with their hands. We take stock of their behavior and its appropriateness to the place and time of day. We listen to their tone of voice and make assumptions about their emotional states and personal facts from what we hear—nervousness, confidence, the gravelly laugh of a smoker, a foreign accent, or a familiar one. If we are physically close enough, we smell perfume and shampoo, we smell the sweat of labor or the sweat of fear. We interpret all these things. We decide who we might extend ourselves to and whose overtures we engage by interpreting all this information. We get *context*. And we use that to choose whom to extend ourselves to, whose overtures we respond to, who to trust with our bodily safety, with our social distance, with our time.

The gaze is not always an innocent probe for friendly interaction, and intentional violations of civility can be harassing and threatening. Stares can be used to draw boundaries, and make clear that those boundaries are going to be protected. In the United States, this happens frequently to black people in predominately white areas, no matter how they're dressed and how they're behaving. Prolonged gazes by men at women are the most minimal end of street harassment, which can escalate into sexualized comments and invitations or even outright menace. Many women experience street harassment repeatedly every day, others weekly or monthly. When surveyed, few women responded that they never experience it. One of the traps for women who are harassed is the general social expectation that questions will be answered, requests either granted or denied (in other words, at least acknowledged), and compliments thanked. In the face of harassment, women's choices are all "rude." They can ignore or confront their harassers by bypassing the social expectations of exchange. They're asked to perform their gender by smiling at the attention they receive. They're expected to take it all as a compliment. Street harassment is defined by the victim. If it feels like harassment, it is. Neutral statements like "Have a nice day" can feel like yet another bit of gendered hassling when your day has been filled with more menacing comments.

They lean against the fences like they own them. They leer as I pass by, scanning my body and hissing, "God bless you, baby," as if the form of a prayer made it all okay, as if it wasn't just another come-on.

If a woman responds as though she is feeling harassed—by ignoring her harassers, using protective body language, back talk—she is being harassed. Whether or not a woman experiences discomfort or feels threatened varies to some degree on the situation, but the fact remains: Violations of civil inattention that aren't respectful are not okay, and aren't going to lead to the feelings of belonging and connectedness I'm talking about. Quite the opposite. These kinds of violations leave people feeling threatened, alienated, objectified, unwelcome, and like public space isn't safe for them.

In Goffman's tidy formulation, an initial gaze is quick so that if it's rejected, no one's feelings get hurt. But it's not always that simple. Researchers studying social gaze have found that an unreturned gaze in both strangers and friends produces significant feelings of ostracism and devaluation. There is a deeper form of nonengagement when the response to a glance is not just a rejection. People can be looked at "as though through air," with a gaze that looks past them, actively withholding actual eye contact. Experiments have shown that this response loudly signals ostracism, as opposed to the returned gaze or smile that signals acknowledgment and inclusion. The passage from Rankine in Chapter Three is a piercing example. Ostracism feels terrible in its own right and provokes self-deprecating questions: Why me? Personality, looks, clothes, class, gender, race, ability, you don't know what it was, and you criticize yourself. Or you harden into hate.

Glances returned and unreturned, overtures accepted and refused, these are moments of true social and emotional risk. It's as essential to be aware of how you reject interaction as it is to pay attention to how you accept it. Civil *attention* matters to the moral fabric and smooth mechanics of society as much as civil inattention does. Remember how strong a force negative experiences are in reversing the positive effects of contact with people different from you? Hold that knowledge with you as you walk through the world of strangers.

• • •

An unobtrusive approach.

Saying Hello

Let's say that instead of the usual averted glance of civil inattention, you want to take a risk, extend yourself to a fellow
human, and say hello. The meaning of greetings can be just as
tangled as those of gazes. Even to say hello in passing may break
the contract in a small way in some cultures, so you're taking a
small risk of intruding. Or failing to say hello may be read as an
affront. Goffman observed that while greeting in passing isn't
part of the norm in the dominant group he studied, for people
he describes as subject to group discrimination, there is often
a sense of solidarity that makes for an expectation of mutual
greeting. Anderson notes that in black culture (in his experience and study), greeting has a special importance. In general,
people who are in the minority in a situation tend to notice

and greet each other: black parents of kids in a majority white school, white parents of kids in a majority black school (it may be more complicated for the kids in both cases), women at a conference mostly attended by men, fathers at a playground where it's most common that the parents and caretakers are women.

In China, as a rule, people don't talk to strangers. According to one scholar, traditional courtesy is reserved for networks of family and insiders. "Strangers, women, peasants, [and] migrant workers" don't get or expect linguistic courtesies. In recent years, she says, the central government has promoted "five courteous phrases" that are European-style equivalents of *hello, please, thanks, sorry*, and *good-bye* to "expand courtesy to universal, reciprocal greetings."

Greetings alone are a meaningful passing acknowledgment that we are all in this together—exchanging a greeting unexpectedly can change the tenor of your day. They're easy and noncommittal—you can greet someone without even slowing down. If the general pace of movement where you are is easygoing, or you're in a stationary moment—waiting for a light to change, walking past a person at rest, in a transitional space—there's a chance that a greeting can open up something beautiful.

They're young and spilling over with winter's pent-up energy, shouting and bouncing and swiping at one another. One's got his hood up, he looks tough. I'm at the corner with them, waiting to cross the street, giving a wide berth to their erratic motion. The one in the hoodie turns to me and says, "It's a beautiful day, right?"

"Sure is," I tell him. His face is narrow, his eyes a little volatile. I shift back just a bit. There's nothing dangerous about him, his body needs some extra space.

He points up at the house-high pear tree in full white bloom across the street. "You see how the trees are coming back to life," he says. "That's God, baby. Ain't no Mother Nature, that's right."

He punches his friend in the meat of his shoulder and they run into the street, racing to cross in the lull between cars, long before the red light comes.

If you want to talk to strangers you have to pick your moments. It should go without saying (but almost never does) that people are more likely to get into conversations when they're not in a hurry. In creating their weird and wonderful technological installations intended to generate public interactions, my students perennially got caught in this problem. They chose busy walkways to install their interaction-prompting projects, hoping that more pedestrians would see them. When people are trying to get from here to there, they don't notice other people and they're far less likely to notice, let alone meet, a gaze. In a crowded place, civil inattention is easy. I asked a friend who says he talks to everyone if he ever refrains. "I guess there is a limit, yeah. I'm not going to interrupt anyone, so if they look busy, or in a hurry, or they're deep in a conversation, I'll pass them by." Looking busy, walking fast, they're good shields against interaction.

Given all these small and large complications, how do you start? There are a few approaches that usually get at least a minimal response, whether or not it rolls into a conversation.

As I said earlier, the general expectation is that questions get answers. Requests are either granted or denied. Compliments lead to thank-yous. These are all low-level demands on someone's time and attention. Remember: Because these types of utterances "require" responses in order not to be rude, they can also be abused—harassment can take the form of continued bids for someone's attention who has made it clear they're not interested.

Compliments, given respectfully, are great levers to open an interaction with a stranger. To give a compliment means that your eyes are open, you are present. You are seeing someone as an individual. Most of the skilled stranger-talkers I know in the United States are practitioners of the art of the compliment.

We were both shifting back and forth, waiting for the slow elevator to come down. He was wearing shoes that looked as though they were never meant to be worn. Laceless low boots of spotless cream fabric, with sculpted creases and artfully frayed edging. I told him they were beautiful.

"Thanks," he said. "Are you in fashion?"

"Not at all," I told him. "I'm in noticing."

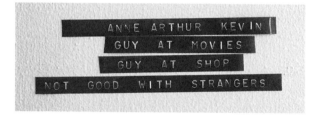

Through a multi-media email exchange, I try to convert a shy friend.

Another easy way to start a conversation is by tossing out casual observations about the shared space you're inhabiting. This is such a slam-dunk method that it sometimes even guides urban development. In their efforts to revive faltering parks and plazas or to construct successful new public spaces, city planners and urban thinkers want their public spaces to be hotbeds of interaction between strangers. They talk about this as a social good. One of their most intriguing strategies is to create points of triangulation. It's deceptively simple. Interactions between strangers increase when there is something to talk about, something to make an observation about, a third thing to close the triangle between the two people who don't know each other. Good public spaces have public art, busking musicians and performers, and food, as well as good places to sit like benches and shallow steps. For me, watching street performers is all about the side conversations even more than it is about enjoying the actual performances. When a public space has things around which to triangulate, it becomes a more open place. If you're in range of something worth commenting on, you may be offered a comment, or choose to make one to the person next to you.

I love it when people are singing to themselves in public, on a park bench or a stoop, while they're working or walking. I get to say, "Sounds great!" or ask what song it is, or just share a little laugh when our eyes meet. They've made themselves a point of triangulation and created an opening for interaction—intentionally or not. You are more likely to be greeted if you're wearing flamboyant clothing in an everyday context, have a dog or a baby, are riding an unusual bicycle, dragging a suitcase,

stopping to look at something, singing, smiling, eating, or waiting. Dogs and babies get commented on: "So cute, how old is she?" or "What kind of dog?" They can also be "social conduits" for people to talk *through*. Speaking first to the dog or baby and not to the owner or caregiver directly is low risk. It's easier for the owner or caregiver to keep moving along without being rude if they don't want to engage than it would be if you spoke directly to them. As a good citizen of public space, it's important to tread lightly when you rely on this kind of approach. People wearing attention-getting hats do not always, in fact, want to get into a conversation about their hats. Some people prefer that their dogs and children be left alone.

Today everyone's talking. The contractor wants to talk about my shoes. "They're good for my back," I tell him. "Usually I slouch." I drop a shoulder forward to show him, and he taps it with one finger. "Bad habits" is all he says.

The butcher likes my scarf. "Emergency purchase," I tell him, "One day it just got cold all of a sudden and I had no choice." He smiles. "That's the only way to shop."

Out on the street a little boy backs up against his mother's legs and stares at me. "Your hair is red," he says. It's true. It's the color of a fire engine. He's terrified.

You can also ask for or offer help. When I see people puzzling over maps on street corners I always ask if they need help. Sure, it's nice to do a good deed, but what really makes me happy is that little connection, or when they start telling me why they're going where they're going, or where they're visiting from and what they've been doing on their trip. Asking for help, for me, is a surprisingly vulnerable experience, and when someone stops to take care of you, even just to help you find your way, it feels very, well, human. I heard from a half-German, half-Egyptian woman who has lived in both countries that in Egypt, a culturally ingrained tradition of hospitality to strangers and travelers means the dynamics of help are fluid and easy—and if you get into a conversation with someone they'll probably invite you to their home. A friend of mine is a researcher who works frequently in Central Asia and East Africa. As a woman traveling alone without any connections, her survival strategy is this: Get one person to see you as fully human and then other people will too. Sometimes all that takes is a smile, but often it comes about when she asks for the help that she genuinely needs.

Help in service situations has its own complex meanings. In the United States, clerks in stores and waiters and other service workers usually see it as part of their job or to their advantage to be friendly and helpful. But their experience is complicated by the consumer transaction inherent in their role. A longtime café proprietor in the southern United States told me, "I have spent my adult life meeting and greeting strangers. I find it fascinating, but it does take its toll on me as well as rejuvenates me. This is such a consumer society that I wonder how sincere I am or if I am being manipulative. To talk to strangers is to cover up but also to care." By contrast, a friend who immigrated to the United States from Russia as a child, and still speaks Russian fluently, told me that when she went back to Russia for a year as an adult, she was struck by "the brusqueness and ab-solute lack of acknowledgment in places of commerce. I could walk into a shop empty of customers and the shop employees (usually women, unsmiling and sullen) wouldn't acknowledge me unless I asked for their attention, which would be granted with bored disinterest. But that's a space of service and trans-action and power, the residue of Soviet times when consumers had no power and shop clerks were gatekeepers to hard-to-come-by goods."

There's one last way to start a conversation, and it runs the risk of being rude, but it's my favorite. You get into all sorts of conversations this way—some last a moment, some last for hours. It amounts to butting into someone's business. Think about performances that happen in theaters, like plays or dance recitals. There is a "fourth wall," the sides and back of the stage form the other three. The pretense is that the actors onstage think they're in a four-sided box, but we can see through the fourth wall. Sometimes, a playwright or choreographer has a character break the fourth wall, address the audience directly, admit they can see us, and force the audience to understand themselves as part of the action. Movies do this sometimes too, with a character addressing the camera directly. So, in public places, you can think of civil inattention as a kind of fourth wall. And you can break it by talking to someone who thinks they are protected by the wall of civil inattention, or by lightly interrupt-ing people who are talking near you as if you weren't there—people who are interacting with each other on the presumption that you'll give them civil inattention. You might be sitting in a café, and the people next to you start laughing uproariously. You heard the funny thing they said too, so you make brief eye contact, laugh with them for a moment, and look away. Or the child at the table next to you is begging for a cookie, and you share a glance with the mother who catches your gaze and rolls her eyes. You smile. It can be more of an intrusion—the risk that might equally lead to a long conversation or a strong rebuke. Imagine you are sitting in a café at the table next to mine, talking with your friend about a movie you just saw, maybe about the special effects. And I lean slightly toward you and say, "That explosion was the scariest thing I've ever seen!" You might scowl at the intrusion. You might laugh and signal that our interaction is over and I should get back to what I was doing. Or you might respond by bringing me into your conversation for a while, by dropping the fourth wall, by forgetting that we're all there separately and instead acting like we're all there together.

Do you see it now? Everything really interesting that happens between strangers begins when you bend invisible rules in positive ways.

• • •

Where the Action Is
There are places that may be thought of as "open" to sociability between strangers. If you enter an open place, the rules of inattention relax. You won't be surprised if a stranger says hello and offers small talk on a public basketball court, in a bar, at a

café, in a public park or square, at a resort or in a hotel lobby, on a cruise ship, at a large party, at a public event like a parade or demonstration, or in a museum. These are places where, more or less, people have chosen to be with the expectation of a generally social atmosphere (though occasionally in spite of it). The delicate dance of civil inattention is not as strict. You will probably have more of a need to ask minor questions, and less prohibition against doing so. Is this seat taken? Do you know where the drinks are? Do you need an extra player? In a relatively populous place where people have gone knowing that they'll be in close quarters, there is not as much need to prove you're not going to seriously impinge on anyone's time, nor is there as strong a need to acknowledge others for courtesy's sake. You can't possibly say hello to everyone in a bar, at a party, or in a lobby. Well, you can, but that would be performance art.

In open places such as cafés you have the twist of how long you're sharing space. You might end up sharing a table with another person—these days mostly while reading or working on a laptop. A barely perceptible negotiation begins when you ask to sit down. It continues as you and that person have a brief, friendly exchange—even a simple smile or nod—and then make it plain that you're going to respect each other's public privacy by going about your business. You're going to be in this together for a while, and the baseline has to be clear and mutual. The only legit trespass is an occasional request to watch belongings while you get more food or use the restroom—although you can take the risk of commenting on a conversation your tablemates are having. As I said, I do this a lot and it's usually a fun exchange.

In any case, in this situation, if the boundaries are not to your liking you can always move or leave.

Then there are situations where you can't really leave—elevators, lines, and modes of transportation. These are transitional spaces, when you're in close quarters with others on your way from here to there. Civil inattention grows more complex to pull off—though failing at it can sometimes take you down interesting roads.

In an elevator the norm is not to talk and not to look at one another. In an elevator you have little control over how long you are in the situation. There are intricate and patterned dances people go through in order to reshuffle physical distances and avoid eye contact as they pack into and exit elevators. It is only when just two or three people are left that one stranger might turn to another and speak. When that happens politely, there's unexpected transformation of the space into an open one and that can change the experience into a moment of connection.

There are also transitional situations created by collective waiting. Waiting rooms, waiting in lines, waiting for things like the arrival of a train or plane that isn't on time. You are in the same powerless shoes as everyone else, and that makes it okay to pass the time with commentary on the situation or to ask for information. There are still rules here, a person must generally respond in some minimally polite way. If they're interested in more conversation, they can strike an open stance with their body. If not, they avert their eyes and turn their body away after a brief acknowledgment. Sometimes this signal isn't taken, and you can see the discomfort mount in the face of a person who is being intruded upon against their will. Again, in a line you can leave, but you probably won't unless the discomfort is spectacular. You joined that line for a reason.

Subways and commuter trains are my favorite transitional spaces. There is the rhythm of motion, stop, motion, the conductor's announcements, the steady churn of people getting on and off. Mostly people don't talk, and then something will happen that breaks open the close distances of people's experience. A point of triangulation such as a funny child, a musician playing for spare change, someone talking to himself, a bunch of rowdy kids. An unexpected and unexplained delay between stops. Any of these can prompt an exchange of glances, shrugged shoulders, amused smiles, or exhalations of frustration. Suddenly, it's a space of interaction.

Shared space on a long-distance bus ride or on a flight, with a longer stretch of contact in cramped quarters, has different and fascinating dynamics. The default for most people is to maintain their social distance. On buses people use a playbook of nonverbal strategies to keep the seat next to them empty as long as possible, and to give it up only to someone who isn't, in the words of interviewees from an ethnographic study, "crazy," "a chatter," or "smelly," among other undesirable things. On a plane you don't have a choice, and you're likely quicker to employ overt signals of disinterest in socializing. What do you do to avoid talking to your seatmate? Things people commonly use as barriers to involvement include reading books and newspapers, earphones, averted eyes, thin smiles followed by averted glances, sleeping or pretending to sleep, and just looking out the window. Once I tried pretending not to speak English, but it got messy when the flight attendants came around.

There's another thing about buses and planes. The interaction between people who know they will not meet again is highly specialized, and these physically close, anonymous, long interludes can also produce a space of deep self-disclosure, which, as we saw in Chapter Two, can create a rapidly intimate experience because it's so common for disclosure to become mutual. Recall that reciprocity is a major factor in the level of disclosure in a conversation, whether it's between spouses or strangers. It's striking and counterintuitive that while strangers do not necessarily reciprocate descriptive information, they do reciprocate disclosure of intimate feelings. No wonder it's a weighty proposition to look up from your book on a plane and engage with your seatmate. Anecdotally, we're more likely to do this on short rides, toward the beginning of a ride when it's possible to close the conversation by turning to one's book or movie or sleep, or toward the end of long rides when the potential time commitment is minimal. We also tend to preserve social distance and privacy by not exchanging names, though occasionally, after a satisfying conversation, people introduce themselves at the conclusion of the interaction to affirm they enjoyed it, as they gather their things to leave the plane.

•   •   •

Exit Strategies

Exits can be the most awkward of all the moments in an interaction with another person, particularly a stranger. How do
you end an interaction? Who has the right to end it? The goal is
to end an interaction at will, but without offending the person
you're stepping away from. Whether we're aware of it or not, we
use physical and conversational cues. When our cues are not
noticed or heeded, it gets weedy pretty fast.

Once it begins, an interaction in an open space has a diam-
eter. In Goffman's study the range in the United States was no
closer than one and a half feet and no farther than three feet
or so. So, too close and it's hard to speak directly to each other,
hard to know where to look or gesture, and might feel so uncomfortable that it makes people back away. Too far and you're
not committed physically to being in the interaction. In a larger
group, people may have to lean in to hear or may be at the edges
of the interaction, and their attention can more easily wander or
switch focus.

If you want to make an exit, you can use your body as a signal.
Beginning in small increments, you can step or lean outside that
interaction zone. Losing eye contact is a signal—a more obvious
and intentional one. Unconsciously, you might get a little jittery,
and that's a signal too. Once you do signal, you hope your partner
is getting the message and will either end the interaction or be
prepared when you do. Sending and receiving the message may
even happen quickly enough that there's an illusion of mutuality.

Words work too. Often all you need is a reason or a friendly
parting line. I have to run; I need to get another drink; do you

know where the bathroom is?; I have to check on my friend; hey, it was nice talking to you; or glancing at your phone and saying that my friend, partner, or babysitter is texting me, things like that. These are reasonable needs that require you to end an interaction. Any of these things may be true, but they work as excuses too. So it's nice to be genuine and warm about it, if you can.

To make a clean exit, you also have to contend with which person has the strongest claim to "leave-taking rights" in the conversation. In general, the person who started the interaction has priority to end it. It's a matter, to some degree, of politeness. The person who started the conversation had a reason. It may have been mere curiosity or friendliness, which only give limited priority in ending the interaction, but if the person who started the conversation had a specific need or agenda, it is in theory theirs to close. The logic here is parallel to what we saw in passing conversations—convention requires that questions are answered, compliments acknowledged, and so on. There is a tacit understanding that you have to make sure the person who started the conversation got what they needed. Just as in passing exchanges, this can be abused and you end up forced to be rude in order to exit. Power matters, too. When there is a real or perceived differential in power or status, the person with more gravitas has the right to end the interaction and may choose to do so politely or not.

So much of this, almost all of it, happens beneath the level of logic and reason. It's all gut, instinct, sensory information, and fantastically subtle cues. In networked spaces—online, in apps, in games—this all goes to hell. The body is missing. Our communication online is mostly asynchronous and displaced. We have more or less the same problems of signaling, perception, and interpretation. Is this safe? Will this person respect reasonable boundaries of contact and propriety? Is this person really who they present themselves as? Does this person want to be greeted? There's no way of being tuned into the other person's level of engagement and no cues for impending endings. We answer these questions differently with non-sensory information. We might look up someone's presence on social media and see what kinds of things the person says in public, we might see if we know any people in common, and whether the person has a generally consistent identity across platforms. How do we figure out things like whether or not a tweet exchange, a comment stream, an IM conversation, or email correspondence concluded? What do you do if someone keeps ending their messages with questions? In person, we can eventually extract ourselves from a conversation without satisfying the person who started it. It's rude, but it can be tempered with a wave and a smile as one walks away. In technologically mediated conversations, "walking away" leaves only silence. We have no gestures of closure. People have been communicating this way for years and still haven't developed many standard cues and behaviors for making online entrances and exits more graceful.

All these solutions to the mechanical problems we face as we share public space, all the implicit rules, bodily expressions, and the words that do and don't come out of our mouths—all of these are things we're only dimly aware of. Learning to see what has been hidden from you carries the thrill of secret knowledge. It's also practical knowledge. It helps you understand when you feel graceful and when you feel awkward as you share spaces and moments with people you don't know. It helps you pull yourself into a transformed social landscape, one that is open and rich with surprising, fleeting, affirming connections. And using this precious and practical knowledge can inch us all toward a more intriguing, respectful, tolerant world.

It's a Fellini movie on the subway this morning, jammed with people who look like out-of-work carnies grown old. That fat Russian man with the thick neck, he's the strongman. I see the flowing orangey locks of a lion tamer reading the newspaper. There's a stout woman with the sparkly makeup of a trapeze flyer. A man whose nose would need little addition to play the clown leans against the door. One woman has a palsied face, her lips and eyes outlined in black, a bearded lady once, certainly. Sitting across from me is a tall dark man, his shaking hands holding a barker's top hat in his lap. I know I'm staring at them. I am filled with wonder that might easily pass for rudeness. The train grinds into the station and the bearded lady gets up to leave. She leans down as she passes me and touches my face. "We were all beautiful once," she says.

On New York City subways things like this happen. But on any given ride, the majority of people are wearing headphones, and so they are mostly isolated from the possibility of interaction. One of my students performed a radical, poetic intervention into that field of isolation. He was listening to music with headphones, sitting next to a woman also wearing headphones, who was moving a little to her music. He took off his headphones and held them out to her. She looked puzzled for a moment, then took hers off and traded with him. They listened to each other's music for a few minutes and then traded back. Not a word passed between them.

He was so thrilled and moved by this experience that he wanted everyone to have it. He tried to think of ways to promote this act of exchange as an urban behavioral meme. He imagined putting stickers all over the subways, he tried creating iconography representing the exchange and showing what to do. In the end it became clearer and clearer that it was impossible. It was too hard to explain so simply the many layers of pleasure involved—the wordless communication, the brief sense of connection, communion made deeper by being wordless, the actual music—and too hard to convey how little risk it really entailed. That being refused or misunderstood is a little awkward, nothing more.

A moment of communion like that isn't common, but you can find little ones when you offer a smile in passing to someone you don't know. For me, this special way of feeling connected to the people I share a world with is essential to my existence. Without it, even when I am immersed in the love of my family and friends, I feel a pinch of loneliness and disconnection. When I feel that way, I hit the sidewalk.

I love the greetings and shared wisecracks and discussions of people's eager dogs. I love telling a story and hearing one. For me, the deepest sense of communion comes from understanding something about a stranger's inner self. If I meet you on the street and we get to talking, I might not just be passing the time and getting a dose of connection. I might be looking for something, a tiny crack I can open and see what you'll show me that's true. I want your spark and your shine and your fissures of imperfection.

Those shimmering moments when I get what I want are rare. Most of the time I just say hello and maybe you say hello back. And then we're here together in this place, you and I. And we are strangers.

Reading is one thing, action another. You can take my word for all this, but why would you? Talking to strangers is a lived experience, calling out to all your senses and your bodily self. You have to go where the action is.

Each of the following expeditions provides a structure and a contrivance to help you explore the world of people you don't know. Each gives you a method or a reason for talking to a stranger, mechanical problems to solve.

You can do them alone or with an expedition partner. In pairs, you each go on separate expeditions and report back as you go along. Take notes with your mind as you go along, and write them down when you get back. I encourage you to share your notes, on your blog, your social networks, anywhere you write about your experiences. You can enlighten your friends and readers with your observations. And documenting experiences is a special way of processing them for yourself. You can do them all in one day or spaced out over months. You might enjoy one of them and do it over and over. You might try this and find it's not for you. Anything is possible.

The guiding principle of these expeditions is respect for others, and every explorer should pay careful attention to their own conduct. If you are male or have a male appearance, be especially respectful when speaking to women and people who have a female appearance, since by default you could be seen as threatening or intrusive. Be polite, keep a bit of extra physical distance, and if people aren't giving you signals that they're open to interaction, don't push it.

Remember the tremendous cultural differences in expectations of eye contact and street behavior. Remember that context matters, as it did in the helping-behavior experiments in Chapter Three, in which, for example, people in Tel Aviv were averse to picking up an unmailed letter. These expeditions may not all make sense in the place where you are. So for these same reasons, I recommend against doing them in cultures you're not steeped in or native to.

The expeditions are presented in order of increasing challenge—increased complexity, increased emotional risk, increased potential for depth of interaction. The first expedition is a warm-up to help you slow down your pace and sharpen your awareness, hone your skills at observing public behavior, and get you in the right frame of mind. I highly recommend you do this once no matter which other expeditions you might choose.

Expedition: "People Watching"

You'll need a notebook for this. Spend one hour in a public place where you are not likely to encounter people you know. Try a park, a café, or a public plaza, a tourist destination, a bus or train. Anywhere you can linger and watch people who are not moving rapidly is perfect. Choose a good place to sit so you'll be able to see a variety of people at a relatively close distance. Sit still. Turn off your devices; get off the grid. I really mean OFF.

It's only an hour—you can do it! Part of the challenge here is full presence.

Start looking around you. First, describe the setting. Where are you? What are the most interesting features of the place? What is it for? What do people do there that it isn't designed for? What kinds of people are there? Take notes on what they look like, how they are dressed, what they do and don't do, how they interact with one another. If there is a big crowd, you can focus on just a few people if you want. If you are inspired to invent backstories for any of them, make sure to specify the details about them that inform your narrative. So, for example, if you conclude that someone is confident or rich, homeless or shy, a tourist or lives in the neighborhood, what told you that? Their posture, their skin, their clothing? Slow down your mind and understand where your assumptions come from.

As an ethnographer, when I return from fieldwork or interviews I try to type up my notes or read through them and make additional notes as soon as possible when I get back. It seals in your experience and gives you a chance to process it with a little distance but while you still remember it clearly. There's no need for you to do this, but if you're savoring the experience, consider it. An equally good way to metabolize what you've experienced is to tell some stories about it to your friends or family.

Expedition: "Say Hello to Everyone"
Take a walk in a populous place like a park with paths or along a city sidewalk. Define a territory for yourself: Are you going to

walk around the block? From the oak tree to the far bench? Give yourself a reasonable territory to traverse, something that will take at least five to ten minutes. Choose a place that has a reasonable density of pedestrians but not a packed pathway. Walk slowly. Your mission is to say hello to every person you pass by. All of them. Try to look them in the eye, but don't worry if they don't hear you or ignore you. You're just getting warmed up.

Now try it again and mix in phatic observations—the kind that mean little overtly but speak of social acknowledgment—in place of greetings, things like "Cute dog," "I like your hat," or "Cold out today!" These acts of noticing pierce the veil of anonymity and create momentary social space.

Keep a keen awareness of the dynamics of each of these micro-interactions. You're behaving a little strangely in public so pay attention to how people respond. You might make a few people uncomfortable, but since you're doing it with everyone and you're not stopping, the discomfort should be minimal. So what's happening when you greet people? Do they smile? Do they laugh? Are they startled? Do they seem uneasy? Do they talk to their companions about what's happening? If you're nervous about your comfort, you can take a friend along. The friend doesn't have to say anything to anyone; they're just there to make you feel safe.

Expedition: "Let's Get Lost"
This expedition is a sequence of requests that get successively more involved as you progress—if you are able to—through each stage. Have some paper and a pen handy and keep your

smartphone tucked away. The first step is to ask someone for directions. If they stop and give you directions, you ask them to draw you a map. If they draw you the map, you ask for their phone number so you can call if you get lost. If they give you their phone number, you call it. A surprising number of people give out their phone number. Over the years that I used this exercise in my classes, only one student ever actually made the call. "I was surprised by how terrifying that last step was," she told me. "How much space we give one another in this crowded city." I encourage you to be brave here.

Take care in choosing a starting place and destination—you may have to try this a few times to find a pair that works well. It can't be too simple to get to, or the map won't seem necessary. But it shouldn't be so complicated that it's too hard to explain.

I created this exercise almost a decade ago, and it's been made a little harder to pull off with the ubiquity of smartphones. You need to appear plausibly unable to navigate without a hand-drawn map or list of directions. Taking the time to draw or write directions is a slight incursion, and this exercise is about incrementally escalating incursions.

This expedition also requires you to lie. Pay attention to how that feels.

Expedition: "The Question"
People talk if you give them the chance to. They talk when you listen. This expedition calls for asking a stranger a disarmingly intimate question and then simply listening to what they say. By "disarmingly intimate" I mean a question that's unexpectedly

real and personal. It's a question that goes to the center of a person's self. It should also be a question that doesn't require an act of remembering. You want something that people can tap into in an immediate, visceral way. My favorite is "What are you afraid of?" A few people say things like spiders and mice and avoid the emotional invitation, but the majority of people go straight to their hearts and tell you about their fears of death, failure, loneliness, and loss—and the things they say are amazing to hear, amazing to have them shared with you. You can come up with your own questions too, and try out more than one.

The structure works like this. It relies on using video or audio recording equipment (you can use your smart phone) to help legitimate the intrusion and give it some logic. The camera is both a contrivance to permit the question and a little bit of mediation that allows people to open up.

You approach someone who is not in a hurry and ask them if you can ask them a question on camera. Some people may be willing to answer you but not on camera—that's fine! The point is the conversation, not the recording. Start recording before you pose your question. Then be quiet. If they ask you to clarify, go ahead, but don't give them any examples of answers. Your job is to listen. If the person seems comfortable talking, you can ask follow-up questions, but don't be too hasty. Give people a chance to fill their own silences. That's often when the magic really happens.

Expedition: "You Don't Belong Here"

This final expedition takes you into deeper, more complex territory. It's the most emotionally risky. Choose a place you don't fit in, where you are in the minority in some way. If you are someone who spends the majority of your time in the minority, this experience may be as common as rain to you, and you may want to skip it. You should be noticeably out of place—perhaps by race, gender, ethnicity, age, ability, membership, appearance, or other categories of difference. The goal here is simply to observe: What are people doing? How are they responding to your presence? You can try engaging and see how that goes. Be aware, be observant, see if you can understand the micro-local assumptions about public behavior and cleave to them.

Obviously, don't put yourself in any danger, don't choose a place where you'd expect to be met with aggression. You may have a wonderful, eye-opening experience. You may feel like you've stepped into a live version of Shared_Studios' Portals. But also prepare yourself: It's possible you'll feel really awful after this expedition. If that happens, you'll have experienced something essential to empathy. What it feels like to be treated as invisible or unwelcome. I do not wish these things for you, but if you feel them, I hope they will change the way you see the world.

ACKNOWLEDGMENTS

Many thanks are due to June Cohen and Michelle Quint at TED for inviting me to write this book, to Michelle for her insightful editing, and to the good people of Simon & Schuster for putting it into the world. I'm also grateful to Julia Rothman for the stunning cover and illustrations.

I've been talking about talking to strangers for a long time. My feelings about talking to strangers and my knowledge of the ins and outs have been vastly enriched by the many people who've shared stories, reflections, excitement, and dread about their experiences with strangers. Special thanks for this to my ITP students (especially Liesje Hodgson who made that phone call and Toby Schachman who traded earphones on the subway), the members of the HC, Beth Kolko, Addie Wagenknecht, Nora Abousteit, Jeff Sharlet, Cameron Caldwell, Karen Barbarossa, Nicola Twilley, Alex Molotkow, Mark Kingwell, Alix Lambert, Dennis Gavin, Lydia Pettis, all the nameless strangers, and pretty much every friend I have.

Jodi Baker and I have been running ideas up and down flag-poles together about strangers and everything else for most of our lives. She read this manuscript twice in its entirety and fragments of it many more than that, arguing, praising, and making it better all along the way. My dear and longtime friend Rachel Devlin offered canny advice on the text, and pushed me to address the hardest things square on. Richard Nash, ever loyal, supportive, and an editor beyond compare, gave me the gift of his scrutiny just when I needed it most. Genya Turovsky offered her keen poet's eye to the prose. I'm also grateful for some smart nudges from Clay Shirky, and Emily May provided guidance and inspiration on the subject of street harassment.

My partner, Bre Pettis, gave me excellent feedback on the manuscript, and he smiles every time I come running home with another giddy tale of a conversation I had with a stranger. I am grateful for his grandly positive enthusiasm for my work and for the ways he challenges me. This book would not have been possible without the loving household participation of my parents, Meryl Stark and John Casella, who took care of us while I was writing, and still do.

WORKS MENTIONED

Fleeting Intimacy

Nicholas Epley and Juliana Schroeder. "Mistakenly Seeking Solitude." *Journal of Experimental Psychology: General* 143:5 (2014), 1980-99.

Gillian Sandstrom and Elizabeth W. Dunn. "Is Efficiency Overrated? Minimal Social Interactions Lead to Belonging and Positive Affect." *Social Psychology and Personality Science* 5:4 (2014), 437-42.

Gillian Sandstrom and Elizabeth W. Dunn. "Social Interactions and Well-being: The Surprising Power of Weak Ties." *Personality and Social Psychology Bulletin* 40 (no. 7) (2014), 910-22.

Kenneth Savitsky, et al. "The Close-ness-Communication Bias: Increases in Egocentrism Among Friends Versus Strangers." *Journal of Experimental Social Psychology* 47 (2011), 269-73.

Mario Luis Small. "Weak Ties and the Core Discussion Network: Why People Regularly Discuss Important Matters with Unimportant Alters." *Social Networks* 35 (2013), 470-83.

Tanya Vacharkulksemsuk and Barbara L. Fredrickson. "Strangers in Synch: Achieving Embodied Rapport Through Shared Movements." *Journal of Experimental Social Psychology* 48 (2012), 399-402.

Arthur Aron, et al. "The Experimental Generation of Interpersonal Closeness: A Procedure and Some Preliminary Findings." *Personality and Social Psychology Bulletin* 23:4 (1997), 363-77.

Sally D. Farley. "Nonverbal Reactions to an Attractive Stranger: The Role of Mimicry in Communicating Preferred Social Distance." *Journal of Nonverbal Behavior* 38 (2014),195-208.

Allison Abbe and Susan E. Brandon. "Building and Maintaining Rapport in Investigative Interviews." *Police Practice and Research* 15:3 (2014), 207-20.

Charles Antaki, et al. "Self-disclosure as a Situated Interactional Process." *The British Journal of Social Psychology* 44 (2005), 181-99.

Kathryn Dindia, et al. "Self-disclosure in Spouse and Stranger Interaction: A Social Relations Analysis." *Human Communication Research* 23(3) (2007), 388-412.

A World Made of Strangers

Leslie A. Zebrowitz, et al. "Mere Exposure and Racial Prejudice: Exposure to Other-race Faces Increases Liking for Strangers of that Race." *Social Cognition* 26:3 (2008), 259-75.

Loren J. Martin, et al. "Reducing Social Stress Elicits Emotional Contagion in Mouse and Human Strangers." *Current Biology* 25 (2015): 326-32.

David Cwir, et al. "Your Heart Makes My Heart Move: Cues of Social Connectedness Cause Shared Emotions and Physical States Among Strangers." *Journal of Experimental Social Psychology* 47 (2011), 661–64.

Robert V. Levine, et al. "Cross-Cultural Differences in Helping Strangers." *Journal of Cross-Cultural Psychology* 32:5 (2001), 543–60.

Robert V. Levine, et al. "The Kindness of Strangers Revisited: A Comparison of 24 U.S. Cities." *Social Indicators Research* 85 (2008), 461–81.

Kurt Iveson. "Strangers in the Cosmopolis," in Ed. John Binnie, et al. *Cosmopolitan Urbanism*. London and New York: Routledge, 2006.

Fiona Kate Barlow, et al. "The Contact Caveat: Negative Contact Predicts Increased Prejudice More than Positive Contact Predicts Reduced Prejudice." *Personality and Social Psychology Bulletin* 38:12 (2012), 1629–43.

Mark Rubin. "The Disproportionate Influence of Negative Encounters with Out-Group Members on Prejudice." https://sites.google.com/site/markrubinsocialpsychresearch/positive-and-negative-experiences-with-members-of-other-groups

Elijiah Anderson. *Streetwise: Race, Class, and Change in an Urban Community*. Chicago: University of Chicago Press, 1990.

Elijiah Anderson. "The White Space." *Sociology of Race and Ethnicity* 1:1 (2015), 10–21.

Claudia Rankine. *Citizen: An American Lyric*. Minneapolis, MN: Graywolf Press, 2014.

Mechanics of Interaction

Erving Goffman. *Behavior in Public Places: Notes on the Social Organization of Gatherings*. New York: The Free Press, 1963.

Erving Goffman. *Interaction Ritual: Essays on Face-to-Face Behavior*. New York: Anchor Books, 1967.

Jane Jacobs. *The Death and Life of Great American Cities*. New York: Random House, 1961.

William H Whyte. *The Social Life of Small Urban Spaces*. New York: Project for Public Spaces, 1980.

Eric D. Wesselmann and Janice R. Kelly. "Cat-calls and Culpability: Investigating the Frequency and Functions of Stranger Harassment." *Sex Roles* 63 (2010), 451–62.

Kimberly Fairchild. "Context Effects on Women's Perception of Stranger Harassment." *Sexuality & Culture* 14 (2010), 191–216.

Mitchell Duneier and Harvey Molotch. "Talking City Trouble: Interactional Vandalism, Social Inequality, and the 'Urban Interaction Problem.'" *The American Journal of Sociology* 104:5 (1999), 1263–95.

James H. Wirth, et al. "Eye Gaze as Relational Evaluation: Averted Eye Gaze Leads to Feelings of Ostracism and Relational Devaluation." *Personality and Social Psychology Bulletin* 36:7 (2010), 869–82.

Eric D. Wesselmann et al. "To be Looked at as Through Air: Civil attention matters." *Psychological Science* 23:2 (2012), 166–68.

Phoebe C. Ellsworth et al. "The Stare as a Stimulus to Flight in Human Subjects: A Series of Field Experiments." *Journal of Personality and Social Psychology* 21:3 (1972), 302–11.

Joshua D. Meadors and Carolyn B. Murray. "Measuring Nonverbal Bias Through Body Language Responses to Stereotypes." *Journal of Nonverbal Behavior* 38 (2014), 209–29.

Mary S. Erbaugh. "China expands its courtesy: Saying 'Hello' to Strangers." *Journal of Asian Studies* 67:2 (2008), 621–52.

Stefan Hirschauer. "On Doing Being a Stranger: The Practical Constitution of Civil Inattention." *Journal for the Theory of Social Behavior* 35:1 (2005), 41–67.

Esther C. Kim. "Nonsocial Transient Behavior: Social Disengagement on the Greyhound Bus." *Symbolic Interaction* 35:3 (2012), 1–17.

ABOUT THE AUTHOR

Kio Stark's previous books are the novel *Don't Follow Me Down* and the independent learning handbook *Don't Go Back to School*. She lives and talks to strangers in Brooklyn, New York.

Kio's TED Talk, available for free at TED.com, is the companion to *When Strangers Meet.*

PHOTO: RYAN LASH / TED

Brené Brown
The Power of Vulnerability
Brené Brown studies human connection — our ability to empathize,
belong, love. In a poignant, funny
talk, she shares a deep insight from
her research, one that sent her on a
personal quest to know herself as well
as to understand humanity.

Kare Anderson
Be an Opportunity Maker
We all want to use our talents to create
something meaningful with our lives.
But how to get started? (And . . . what
if you're shy?) Writer Kare Anderson
shares her own story of chronic
shyness and how she opened up her
world by helping other people use
their own talents and passions.

Hannah Brencher
A Love Letter to Strangers
Hannah Brencher's mother always
wrote her letters. So when she felt
herself bottom into depression after
college, she did what felt natural —
she wrote love letters and left them for
strangers to find. The act has become
a global initiative, The World Needs
More Love Letters, which rushes
handwritten letters to those in need
of a boost.

Celeste Headlee
10 Ways to Have a Better Conversation
When your job hinges on how well you
talk to people, you learn a lot about
how to have conversations — and that
most of us don't converse very well.
Celeste Headlee has worked as a radio
host for decades, and she knows the
ingredients of a great conversation:
Honesty, brevity, clarity, and a
healthy amount of listening. In this
insightful talk, she shares ten useful
rules for having better conversations.
"Go out, talk to people, listen to
people," she says. "And, most impor-
tantly, be prepared to be amazed."

The Laws of Medicine
Field Notes from an Uncertain Science
by Siddhartha Mukherjee

Essential, required reading for doctors and patients alike: A Pulitzer Prize-winning author and one of the world's premiere cancer researchers reveals an urgent philosophy on the little-known principles that govern medicine—and how understanding these principles can empower us all.

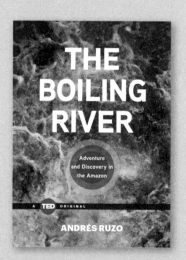

The Boiling River
Adventure and Discovery in the Amazon
by Andrés Ruzo

In this exciting adventure mixed with amazing scientific discovery, a young, exuberant explorer and geoscientist journeys deep into the Amazon—where rivers boil and legends come to life.

The Art of Stillness
Adventures in Going Nowhere
by Pico Iyer

In a world beset by the distractions and demands of technology, acclaimed travel writer Pico Iyer reflects on why so many of us are desperate to unplug and bring stillness into our lives.

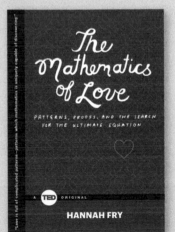

The Mathematics of Love
Patterns, Proofs, and the Search for the Ultimate Equation
by Hannah Fry

In this must-have for anyone who wants to better understand their love life, mathematician Hannah Fry pulls back the curtain and reveals the hidden patterns—from dating sites to divorce, sex to marriage—behind the rituals of love.

ABOUT TED

TED is a nonprofit devoted to spreading ideas, usually in the form of short, powerful talks (eighteen minutes or less) but also through books, animation, radio programs, and events. TED began in 1984 as a conference where Technology, Entertainment, and Design converged, and today covers almost every topic— from science to business to global issues—in more than one hundred languages. Meanwhile, independently run TEDx events help share ideas in communities around the world.

TED is a global community, welcoming people from every discipline and culture who seek a deeper understanding of the world. We believe passionately in the power of ideas to change attitudes, lives, and, ultimately, our future. On TED.com, we're building a clearinghouse of free knowledge from the world's most inspired thinkers—and a community of curious souls to engage with ideas and one another, both online and at TED and TEDx events around the world, all year long.

In fact, everything we do—from the TED Radio Hour to the projects sparked by the TED Prize, from the global TEDx community to the TED-Ed lesson series —is driven by this goal: How can we best spread great ideas?

TED is owned by a nonprofit, nonpartisan foundation.